SMOCKING
DESIGN

JEAN HODGES

SMOCKING
DESIGN

B. T. BATSFORD LONDON

© Jean Hodges 1987
First published 1987
This paperback edition published 1990
Reprinted 1995

ISBN 0 7134 6344 9

Typeset by Servis Filmsetting Ltd, Manchester
and printed in Great Britain by
The Bath Press,
Avon
for the publishers
B. T. Batsford Ltd
4 Fitzhardinge Street
London W1H 0AH

Contents

Acknowledgement

I would like to extend grateful thanks to all those people, too numerous to name, whose interest and enthusiasm have helped during the preparation of this book, and in particular to those who have so generously undertaken commissions or loaned work for inclusion.

My special thanks must go to Ron Head for the photography; Ros Chilcot for the sketches from her notebook; members of the Smocking Group of the Embroiderers' Guild; students from Godalming Adult Education Centre and Hampton School of Needlework; my family for their love, constant encouragement and help in moments of despair; and to my husband, Frank, who could always find just the right word to use when my mind went blank.

INTRODUCTION

In its simplest form, as seen in traditional smocks, the technique of smocking is a practical way of controlling fullness by means of stitchery over gathers, yet it is possible to use smocking as a decorative art in its own right. It is a method of manipulation, of altering the tonal quality, adding to the colour and also changing the weight of the fabric. Dramatic textural effects can be created, and for these reasons smocking has become an exciting and adaptable technique. It is considered by many to be one of the easiest and prettiest forms of embroidery, and is highly rewarding – once a few basic stitches have been mastered.

It evolved in England and Wales as a means of giving freedom of movement and stretch across the back, chest and sleeves of countrymen's smocks. (The smock does not appear to have been adopted in Ireland or Scotland.) The stitching started in a simple way as a means of controlling the fullness of fabric. Initially, one basic form of stitchery was used. This original stitch was called 'rope stitch', and is now known as 'outline stitch'. It is worked in a similar way to stem stitch in surface embroidery. Cable and wave stitch were then introduced, as was feather stitch. The decorative effect of the stitchery was found to be an added bonus to the practical purpose of the smocking. Many interesting variations

1 *Linen smock, 1890, with tape lace and cutwork collar and cuffs.* (By kind permission of the Dorset County Museum. Photograph: Muriel Best)

2 *Detail from fig. 1. The tape lace and cutwork cuff extends below the traditional cuff of the smock. (By kind permission of the Dorset County Museum. Photograph: Muriel Best)*

3 *Panel from a linen round smock thought to have been made in the late nineteenth century. Outline, surface honeycomb and triple feather stitch have been used. (The Smocking Group of the Embroiderers' Guild Collection. Photograph: Andrew Hodges)*

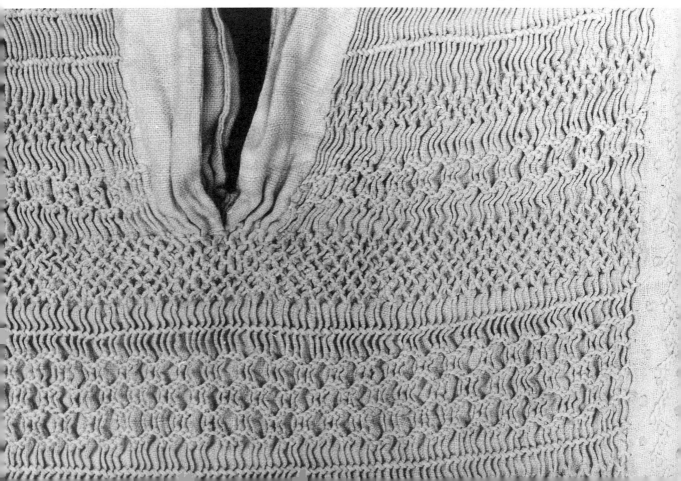

have since been developed to give additional beauty. The wide diversity of smocking as we now know it forms a vital part of our embroidery heritage.

The majority of smocks and garments to be found in museums and private collections show smocking with the same stitch running from the beginning to the end of the row. A number of these single stitch rows were built up into rich textured patterns, yet the garments remained extremely practical. Figs 1 and 2 show a smock of the Art Nouveau period in the Dorset County Museum, with the unusual addition of tape lace and cutwork collar and cuffs. The garment is cut on the lines of a dress, with a gathered head to the set-in sleeves, rather than the traditional smock cut from rectangular pieces which is generally to be found.

4 *Section of a sampler dated 1930, showing how designs can be created by varying the type of stitch used within a row.* (The Embroiderers' Guild Collection)

Fig. 3 shows a typical 'round' smock made from linen and thought to have been worked in the late nineteenth century. This type of smock is cut from rectangles of fabric and is identical back and front – a very useful feature when the front became dirty or worn, as it could then be turned back to front without any problems! The smocking is in deep bands of diamond stitch and triple feather stitch interspersed with outline stitch. There are small areas of smocking at the top of the sleeve and above the cuff. The collar, yoke, 'boxes' (the flat panels either side of the main smocking) and cuffs are embroidered with feather stitch in a simple linear design.

Gradually, smocking became a little more adventurous and a variety of stitch rows were combined to form designs. Traditional countrymen's smocks retained their simplicity, while the more complicated designs were introduced into children's clothing and the fashion world. During the 1880s, fashion catalogues started to display many articles

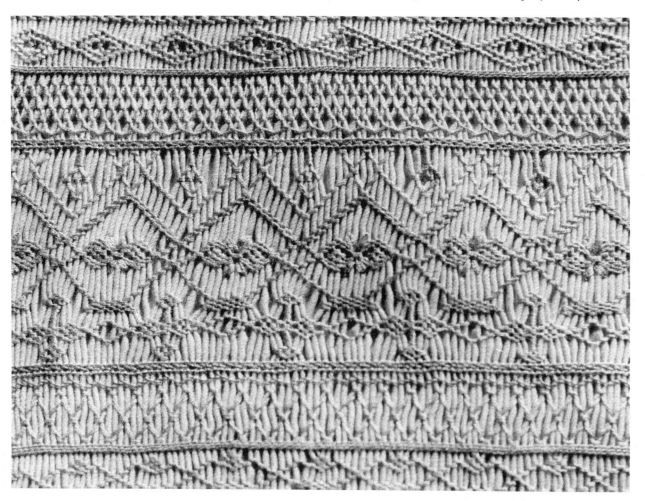

5 *Child's short sleeved smock of about 1930,*
with Dorset wheel buttons and buttonhole loops.
(The Embroiderers' Guild Collection)

6 *Pocket worked as a sample for the City and Guilds Certificate in 1959, the first year the examination was held in Scotland.* (Mary Timms)

which included smocking. Printed instructions for working the technique also began to appear. In these newer applications, greater versatility was achieved by incorporating a number of different stitches within a single row and by building up blocks of pattern. The use of smocking was thereby extended to a wide variety of articles not previously associated with the technique. The result has been the exciting and free artistic use of smocking, not only on clothing but also in panels and wall hangings, which we find today.

7 *Front and sleeve top of a 1986 smock frock. Blue and white Danish flower threads worked on dress weight denim-look polyester/cotton fabric.* (Helen Waycott)

9 *Detail of fig. 8.*

8 *'Coral'. Three-dimensional panel dated 1985. Strips of organza, silk and fine furnishing fabric have been smocked using outline and cable stitch. The strips were then twisted and applied to a lightly padded background fabric.* (Gillian Jenkins)

1 GETTING STARTED

FABRIC TYPES

A wide variety of fabrics such as silk, cotton, cotton/polyester, wool, wool mixtures, fine jersey, satin, synthetics and fine leather can be successfully used for smocking, as experimentation will soon show. All that is necessary is that the chosen fabric should hold the gathers well so that the tubes do not flatten, bubble or distort. Where the smocking is to be incorporated into fashion, it is also essential that the fabrics are soft, pliable, will drape well and will be of a suitable thickness and type for the style of garment to be made. If the style requires a lot of fullness, choose a lightweight fabric, since this will drape well and mould to the body. Sheer fabrics such as chiffon, organza, georgette and voile will also smock beautifully; they do require expert handling, however. A fine thread should be used, and the stitches need to be very accurately and neatly placed. To retain the delicate effect of the fine fabric, the more open and lacy smocking stitch combinations such as diamond or trellis are advisable. Heavier-weight fabrics such as satin, needlecord, velvet and double jersey will also smock effectively, but for these materials a deeper tube should be used and a firmer stitch such as honeycomb or triple honeycomb is recommended to hold the gathers firmly and emphasize the contours.

New fabrics are constantly appearing in the shops, so be prepared to experiment as interesting results can be obtained with the most unconventional fabric. The play of light on the ripples and folds of gathered shot organza, shot silk, heavy satin or panne velvet can be exploited in a variety of exciting ways for hangings, panels and three-dimensional objects. Binca canvas, hessian and hand- or machine-knitted fabrics can produce highly textured results when smocked and should also be considered when working freely.

10 'Summer Garden'. Centre for a herb cushion. White voile smocked in pinks and green, using a fine silk sewing thread. (Jean Hodges)

PATTERNED FABRICS

Squares

These can be smocked very effectively. A beginner will find that gingham provides an ideal way to learn the technique and experiment with the different kinds of stitches. No dots are required, as the fabric can be gathered by using the squares as a guide. Much depends on the arrangements of the checks, but it is possible to highlight a lighter or darker effect of the overall colour by the way in which the gathers are arranged. If the stitches pick up the corners of each square a harlequin effect of mixed colours is created. Picking up the centre of each square gives a bold effect by suppressing the greyed colour and emphasizing the dark and light diamond shapes. If the centre of the light square is picked up, the dark square will come forward (fig. 11); if the centre of the dark square is picked up, the light colour will be emphasized (fig. 12). This highlighting of the dark or light squares can be particularly effective when the smocking is done in a matching thread using honeycomb, surface honeycomb or vandyke stitch.

Experimentation will soon show how easy it is, using only simple stitches, to create a wide range of imaginative ideas and three-dimensional effects.

11 *Surface honeycomb stitch worked on gingham. Picking up the centre of a white square when gathering brings the dark squares forward.* (Sheila Jolly)

12 *Alternating rows of shallow and deep vandyke stitch on gingham can create interesting effects.* (Sheila Jolly)

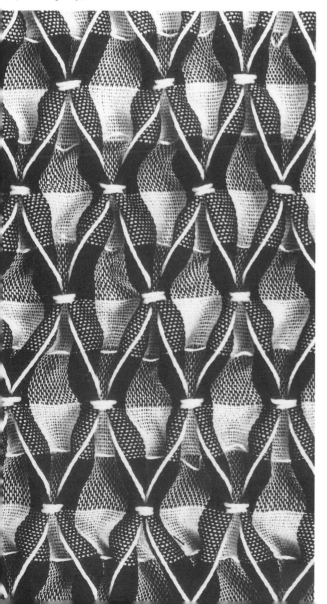

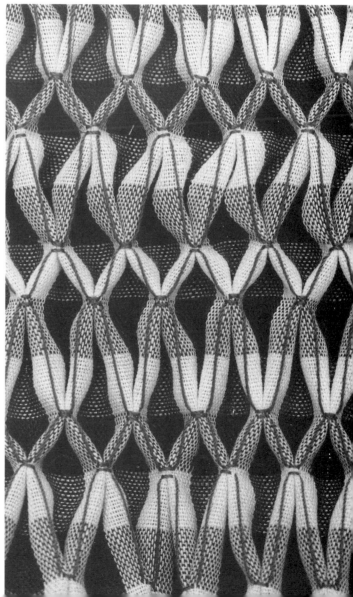

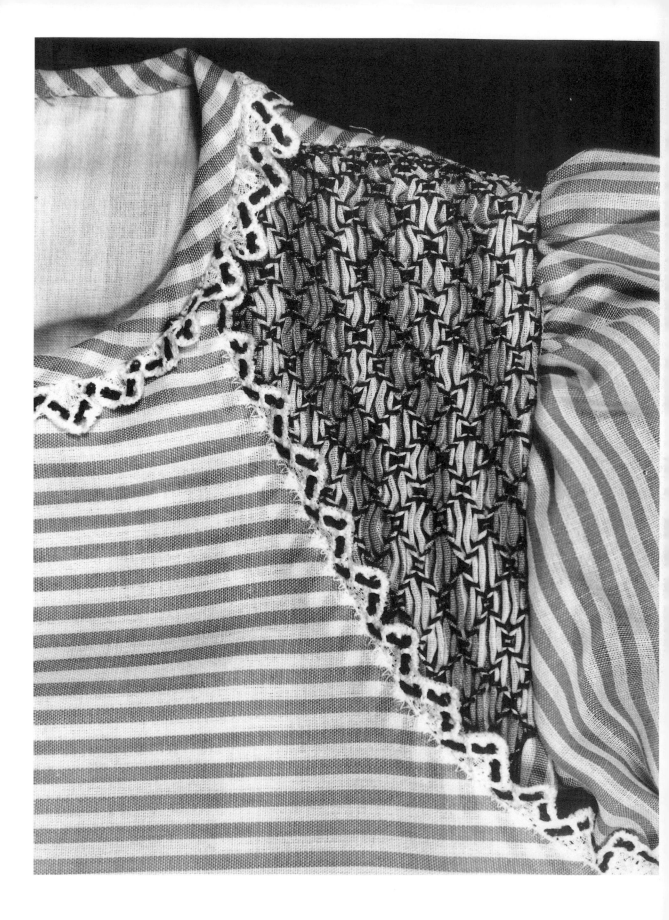

Stripes

Striped fabric can be smocked with great versatility. For example, panels can be set in with the stripes running in different directions to bring out a special design feature. Honeycomb smocking worked over the lighter of the two stripes will give a strong three-dimensional look. When using an evenly striped fabric in this manner, it may be found quicker and easier to bring the stripe forward if the gathering thread is stitched from stripe to stripe instead of picking up a small quantity of the fabric at each dot. To do this, insert the needle into the fabric on the edge of one stripe and bring it out at the edge of the next until the row is complete. To keep the row level, a fine line is first drawn with a sharp, soft pencil on the reverse of the fabric, unless the fabric grain can be clearly followed. An uneven stripe can be very exciting when the gathers are picked up evenly, as blocks of colour will appear, giving wider scope for pattern variations.

Spots

Spotted fabric should be used only if the spots are woven into the fabric on the straight of the grain. Printed spots rarely run true to the grain. If the fabric being used for a garment has the spots running off the grain and they are used for gathering, the fabric will be inclined to pull to one side, no matter how slight the imperfection. Where printed spot fabrics have to be used, to avoid the possibility of distortion it is better to ignore the spots and gather on the straight of the grain. The spots will then make an interesting random pattern of their own which could be incorporated into the overall design.

To bring spots to the surface on the front of a woven material, the fabric should be gathered on the wrong side, picking up on either side of each spot (fig. 15).

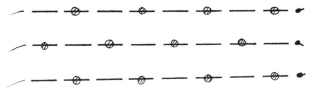

15 *Bringing the spots forward to the right side when gathering spotted fabric.*

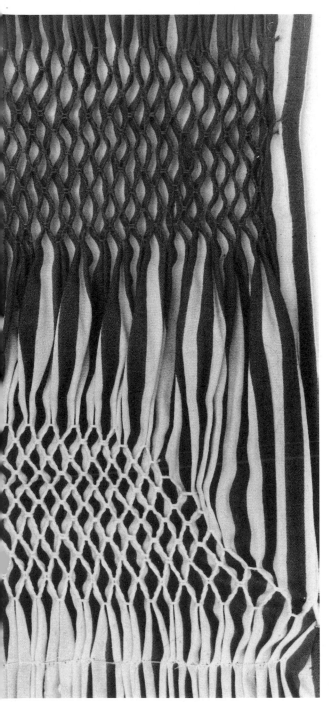

13 (Left) *When striped fabric is put through a gathering machine the stripes can become distorted. This distortion has been used to advantage on the shoulder of a child's dress.* (Rose Glennie)

14 *Either the light or the dark stripe can be brought forward, as shown in this sample.* (Margaret Robertson)

USING PATTERNED FABRICS

Patterned fabrics can be successfully used for smocking, but it must be remembered that when an all-over patterned fabric is gathered, both the pattern and the colour will change. A large floral design can look quite abstract when gathered; a spotted or small regular pattern may appear as horizontal or irregular stripes. The work can take on a greyed or hazy effect due to the shadows created by the tubes; a secondary colour may become dominant because the way in which the fabric is gathered distorts the original colour scheme. Sometimes the result can be so unexpected and exciting that the opportunity for a new approach becomes apparent. It is therefore a good idea to work a sample first and to choose the thread for smocking after the fabric is gathered. Time and

a little extra money spent purchasing a 20 cm (8 in.) sample of the proposed fabric at this stage may prevent future disappointment.

Too many colours can cause confusion and loss of impact on a patterned fabric, so limit the choice of threads to one, or at the most, two. The main colour should generally be a lighter or darker tone of one of the colours within the fabric, with perhaps a contrast used carefully in small areas. When the general background colour of the fabric is light, a dark-coloured thread may make the most impact, whereas a light thread would show up better on a dark background. A simple all-over stitch such as surface honeycomb, diamond or trellis is more suitable than a complicated design which could disappear into the background. Areas of additional colour can be included by means of small flowerettes, bullion knots or satin stitch blocks if necessary.

A very effective way of dealing with a patterned fabric is to insert a panel of plain fabric, smocked in colours found within the pattern. This can be particularly attractive when used on the bodice of a child's dress (fig. 16). If the skirt is to fall in gathers

16 *White lawn smocked in pink, jade and white coton à broder has been inserted into the bodice of a floral print dress. Bullion knot rosebuds and overstitching on the edge of the collar balance the design.* (Karenann Couper)

below the insert, the seam should be opened flat where the two fabrics meet. A piece of narrow elastic held by means of herringbone stitch across the back of this seam will hold the tubes in place. The fabrics can be joined before gathering if a lot of fullness in the skirt is required. On the other hand, if the piece is to be treated as an insertion (see page 51), join the fabrics after completing the smocking, using the bottom gathering thread as the guide. The join line can be softened if necessary by taking some of the smocking stitches over the actual join, or by the addition of surface embroidery, should this be more appropriate.

AMOUNT OF FABRIC REQUIRED

Calculating the correct amount of fabric required for a specified width of smocking is not easy, since a number of contributory factors are involved, namely:

1 the thickness and type of fabric being worked;
2 the distance between the dots which governs the depth of each tube;
3 the thickness of the thread used for the actual smocking;
4 the type of stitches being used (in particular, whether they are firm or stretchy) and the amount of stitchery being used, i.e. a closely packed design will not stretch as much as a very open one;
5 the tension of stitching used by the individual worker.

It will be seen, therefore, that whilst three and a half to four times the amount of the finished width may be a useful general guide, it is necessary to work on a sample using the same fabric, thread and spacing of dots as those chosen for the finished article. Up to six times the width may be required in some cases. Before working the sample, measure across the panel of smocking dots with the material stretched out flat, then check the measurement again after the sample has been completed and the gathering threads removed. The number of dots in the sample can then be multiplied to fit the final width and depth of smocking required.

Loss of depth

The depth of the finished sampler should also be checked, as all smocking takes up a certain amount of the length of the fabric, depending on the stitch and number of rows worked. It is important to take this into account, especially where the size of a finished piece of work is critical, for example in a garment.

FABRIC PREPARATION

Before starting work it is necessary to prepare the fabric. First pre-shrink it, if it is not guaranteed pre-shrunk. To pre-shrink cotton or other washable fabric, immerse it in hot water for about half an hour, drip dry and then press. For wool, wet a sheet and place it on a flat surface, lay the fabric on the sheet, roll them together and leave overnight. Unroll the fabric, leave it to dry and press it if necessary using a steam iron or damp pressing cloth. Once any necessary pre-treatment has been carried out, straighten the grain of the fabric by tearing or cutting along a thread so the ends are at right angles to the selvedge. Cut off the selvedges and press to remove any creases. If the fabric is likely to fray, protect the edges by hand oversewing or zigzag on a sewing machine.

THREADS

Gathering thread

The thread used for gathering needs to be strong, of good quality and in proportion to the weight of the fabric. Sewing cotton and polyester/cotton No. 40 are suitable for light- to medium-weight fabrics; buttonhole twist for very heavy fabrics. Running the thread through a piece of beeswax will help prevent it twisting and tangling when using long lengths. Choose a contrasting colour for the gathering thread but avoid very dark colours, as they can mark light fabrics. The contrasting thread will be visible at the bottom of each tube and act as a guide for keeping the rows of smocking straight.

Working thread

The working thread used for the actual smocking should be in keeping with the background fabric, for example, natural thread on natural fabric, and synthetic on synthetic. Generally, a fine thread is used on a fine delicate fabric, whilst a heavy thread is used to give a bold effect on a thick fabric. However, very interesting effects can be achieved by experimenting with these general rules and varying the type and thickness of the thread.

Twisted threads such as perlé No. 5 and No. 8,

coton à broder and silk or polyester buttonhole twist are recommended for general use, as they are strong and less likely to shred than the stranded variety. The stitches made with these threads will stand out with a crisp, well-defined finish. Where a stranded thread is used, however, experiment with the number of strands required (three or four are generally used on light- to medium-weight fabric); once the gathering threads are removed and the stitches stretched the thread will appear finer. Crochet and tatting cotton, lurex, knitting and fancy yarns can also be considered, whilst experimentation with more unusual threads, ribbons and leather thonging can produce exciting results. Variegated and space dyed threads are very effective and create their own patterns. Do, however, check if using home-dyed threads, that they are colour-fast. Several types and thickness of thread can be combined in the same piece of work to give added interest, especially where a highly textured and decorative effect is required. If a stranded thread is used, try to keep the strands together with the stitches lying smoothly. Sometimes these threads will twist and tangle during stitching. Should this happen, hold the loose end of the thread and run the needle down to the work, release the thread, run the needle back up again and the thread will untwist. When a highly twisted thread becomes untwisted, allow the needle to hang down and the weight will cause the thread to retwist and straighten.

NEEDLES

Crewel (embroidery) needles are used, as they have long eyes, enabling the embroidery threads to pass through easily. They are generally available in assorted packets containing sizes 3 to 9 or 5 to 10. If buying single size packets, 7, 8 or 9 may be found to be the most useful.

Beading needles are helpful for adding beads. They are long and fine and will pass easily through all sizes of beads.

PREPARATION FOR GATHERING

Smocking is worked on tubes formed by parallel rows of gathering stitches, with every stitch lying exactly beneath the one on the row above. Gathering is often considered the most laborious stage of preparation. However, it is most important that it should be carried out accurately. No amount of time or perfection in technique at the smocking stage will overcome an inadequately controlled or distorted panel of tubes.

Most smocking is worked on the straight grain of the fabric. When dots of any kind are being used to aid the gathering process, they are placed on the wrong side of the fabric. A good seam allowance should always be left, and an extra row of dots added at the top and bottom to give added control to the gathers. These extra gathering threads can then be used as the seam line when making up the article.

There are a variety of ways of marking dots and grids to gather the fabric. These include the use of transfers, tissue paper, templates and dressmaker's carbon paper. It is also possible to introduce an element of mechanization by using one of the smocking machines now available. The method chosen to prepare the gathers will depend on the type of fabric being used as well as on individual preference.

Smocking dot transfers

A range of different size and colour smocking dot transfers are available, and should be chosen with the fabric and finished effect in mind. Closely spaced dots giving small shallow tubes are suitable for fine fabrics; widely spaced dots giving deeper tubes are needed for heavier fabrics. As a rough guide, 6 mm ($\frac{1}{4}$ in.) dots are suitable for use on lightweight polyester/cottons, lawn or silk.

The dots are applied with a hot iron to the wrong side of the fabric. Cut the fabric on the grain and press it smooth. Cut away any writing from the transfer and test this on a small scrap of the chosen fabric to check the temperature at which the iron should be set and to make sure the dots do not come through on to the right side of the fabric, as this could ruin a piece of work. The test piece is very important and should also be used to make sure the transfer will wash out.

Lay the fabric, right side down, on the ironing board. Cut the sheet of dots to the required width and depth and lay it wax side down on the wrong side of the fabric. Pin in position, making sure the dots run along the straight of the grain. Set the iron to the correct temperature and press each area for about 10 seconds. Do not rub the iron over the transfer, as this can smudge the dots. Lift a corner of the paper to check the dots have transferred properly before peeling away completely.

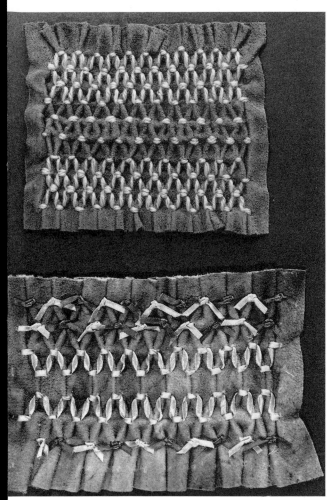

Templates
To make a template, first either rule a grid or glue graph paper on to a piece of thin card. Holes are then pushed through at the intersections, using a thick needle; these may be enlarged with a fine knitting needle or stiletto. When ready, place the template along the straight grain on the wrong side of the fabric and mark dots through the holes, using a sharp pencil and moving the template along as required. This is a useful method for small areas and the template can be used many times.

Graph paper and dressmaker's carbon
For this method, first place a sheet of dressmaker's carbon paper shiny side down on the wrong side of the fabric. (Ordinary office carbon paper should not be used, as it tends to smudge and leave dirty marks.) Next, lay graph paper or a ruled grid over the carbon and pin it in position through all the layers. Placing the pinned layers on a hard surface such as glass or laminate, the dots can be marked using a blunt needle, hard pencil or ballpoint pen.

Gathering machines
There are special gathering machines on the market which may be worth consideration if a great deal of fine smocking is to be undertaken. They do, however, have their limitations. The depth of tube cannot be altered and is set at approximately 6 mm ($\frac{1}{4}$ in.), which may be too fine to hold heavier fabrics in well-defined gathers. The machine also may not take very closely woven fabrics without the risk of breaking some of the needles. These machines can, however, be a great advantage when gathering very fine fabrics such as lawn, voile, chiffon or organza. They are also very useful for experimental work. Before using the machine, the selvedges should be removed from the fabric. The fabric is then laid on a table, right side down, and rolled on to dowelling prior to gathering (fig. 19). When feeding the fabric through the machine, care should be taken to ensure that the gathering remains on the straight of the grain. It is easier to keep the fabric straight if it is held in place on the dowel along the edge of the fabric by strips of masking tape. Do remember, however, to remove the tape before the end is reached – machines do not like sticky tape!

Interesting shadowy effects can be achieved by laying pieces of chiffon, organza or similar fine fabrics on the main material as it passes through the machine, provided it does not become too thick. The main fabric remains on the straight of the

17 *Vandyke stitch using wool and fine ribbons on soft leather.* (Mary Fortune)

Tissue paper
This method is recommended to avoid marking or damaging delicate fabrics and for multi-coloured prints where dots would not show up easily. Plot the dots or rule a grid pattern to the required width and depth on to tissue or greaseproof paper. Tack or pin the paper to the wrong side of the fabric, making sure the dots run straight across the grain of the material. Gather the dots directly through the paper. When all the gathering is complete, score along the lines of stitching with a needle and carefully tear the paper away. This is a particularly versatile method, as it leaves no marks if you decide to smock a smaller area than originally planned, or when a panel is to finish with points.

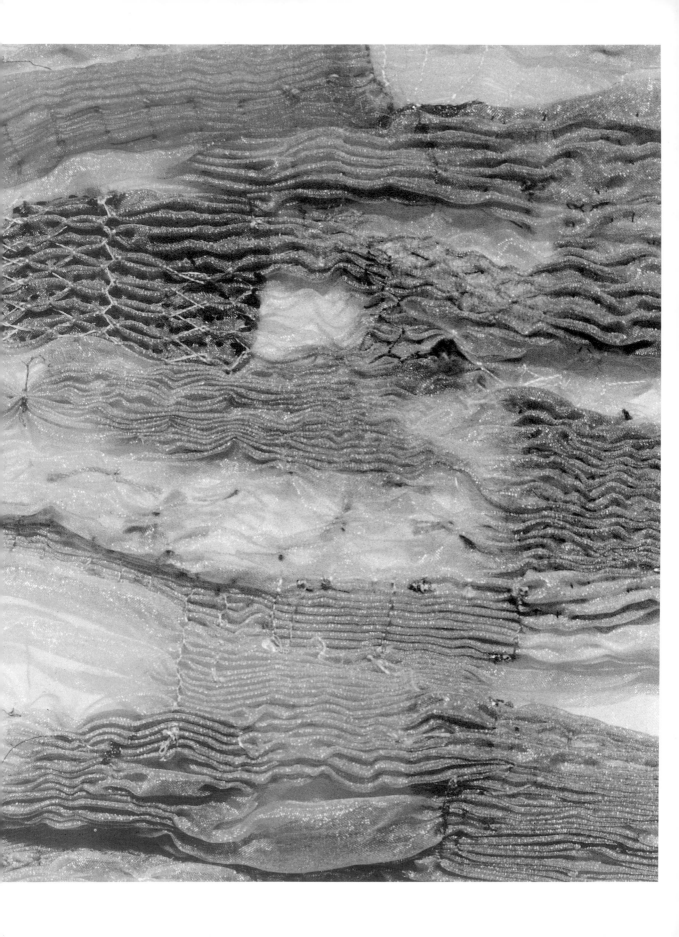

18 *Sample of various fine fabrics put through a gathering machine one after the other, noting how each reacts to give a patchwork of colour and texture. This idea could be developed in a variety of ways for use in panels, wall hangings or evening clothes.* (Toni Gardner)

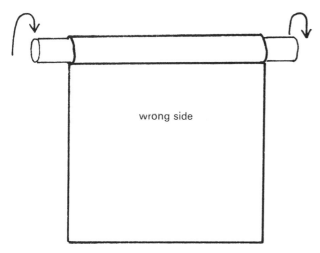

wrong side

end to be fed into machine

19 *Rolling fabric on to dowelling prior to gathering.*

grain, but the additional pieces can lie in any direction, depending on the required effect. Fine whisps of fleece or wadding can also be fed through to give a misty or cloudy appearance.

GATHERING BY HAND

When preparing to gather, select a suitable thread in a contrasting colour (see page 19) which is long enough to measure across the row of dots plus an extra 10 cm (4 in.). Work on the back of the fabric, using a separate thread for each row. Start with a very large knot in the thread. A small backstitch can

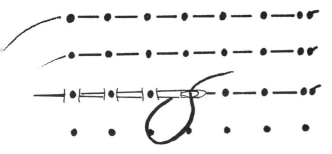

20 *Picking up the dots.*

also be made if the fabric is very fine, but this is not generally necessary. Work from right to left (left to right for left-handed embroiderers), picking up a small amount of fabric at each dot. The stitches should be as even as possible to keep the tubes of equal depth. The fabric can be slid up the needle and a number of stitches taken at one time. The spare thread is left hanging at the end of each row. Work all the rows, remembering to add an extra one at the top and bottom of the panel. These will be used in making up the article.

Pull up the gathering threads in pairs, working all the way down the panel so that it is loosely gathered. Leave the threads hanging at this stage. Always push the fabric up the thread rather than pulling the individual threads through the fabric, which can cause strain and breakage.

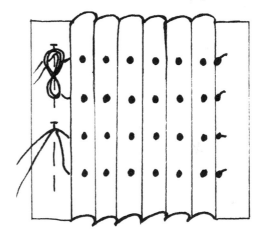

21 *Threads pulled up in pairs and wrapped round a pin.*

Once the whole panel has been loosely drawn up, return to the top, and again taking the threads in pairs, pull the gathers up to make the tubes close, but not so tight that they will not move easily. Wrap the threads, still in pairs, in a figure of eight around a pin which has been inserted where the threads emerged. As a very rough guide to a suitable tension, when working over an area of approximately 90 cm (36 in.), pull the gathers tight, then, placing the first finger and thumb of the right hand on the thread about 10–12 cm (4–5 in.) away from the last tube, ease the gathers along to where the thread is being held before wrapping around the pin. This will give an idea of a suitable tension to work from. Stroke down the tubes on the front and back with the eye of a needle to help set the tubes in a straight line. When a springy fabric is being used, it may help to steam the tubes at this stage to make them more defined.

Difficulty may be encountered in drawing up each gathering thread to the same length when a large area of smocking is to be worked. To overcome this problem, pin the knotted (right-hand) side of the panel on to an ironing board or similar surface so as to provide a firm straight line, thus enabling the tubes to be pulled up to an equal length.

SMOCKING ROUND CURVES

As already stated, smocking is normally worked on the straight of the grain. There are occasions, however, where a specific fashion detail is being used which requires a slight curve, such as at the neck of a dress or set below a curved yoke on a coat or blouse. If only a very slight curve is needed, the gathering threads can be graded to accommodate it. A fuller curve will need the dots to be carefully slashed and widened slightly, as shown in fig. 22. Provided closely spaced dots are used, the tubes at the bottom of the curve should not become too wide to cause problems when smocking.

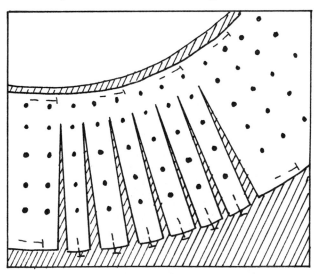

22 Slashed and spread pattern of dots to fit round a curve.

An easier, and often more effective, result can be produced by ignoring the curve, cutting the fabric out on the straight of the grain and gathering in the normal way. The choice of stitches can then cause the fabric to curve. Firm, closely worked stitches are used at the narrowest part to control the gathers. Gradually, as it is worked down, the pattern can become more decorative and open, ending with deep waves or points to give the most stretch. The child's dress shown in fig. 26 and the collars in figs 24 and 25 are good examples of working on the straight of the grain and allowing the stitch design to form the curve.

When working a curve on a straight-cut neckline, it is best to apply the dots whilst the fabric is flat and before joining the seams. To ensure that the fabric will be evenly gathered and the seamline unobtrusive, the vertical row of dots should be placed on the seamline – a small adjustment can be made to the seam allowance if necessary. The curve of the sleeve must, therefore, start after the last row of dots. Match the dots carefully at the row endings to make sure the seam will run exactly through the middle of

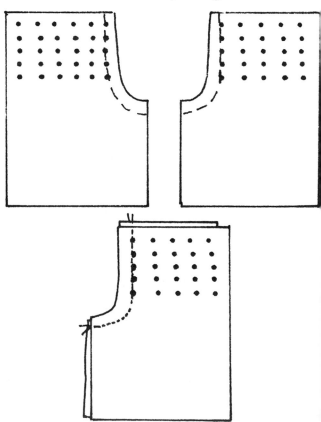

23 Armhole seam running through a straight row of dots.

24 Child's collar. Cable and wave stitch worked on a straight length of broderie anglaise, with the neck edge covered with bias binding. (Heather King)

25 Collar. Two widths of white voile joined with a fine French seam, then gathered on the straight of the grain and smocked in two shades of blue coton à broder. The wave stitch takes on a curved appearance as it is spread out. (Jean Hodges)

26 *Child's dress. Diagonally worked surface honeycomb stitch, using a rainbow of pastel colours, creates a curved appearance on a straight-cut neckline. The seams were joined before the fabric was gathered on a gathering machine. Narrow ribbon threaded through the bottom edge of the smocking completes the design.* (Heather King)

the dots (fig. 23). Join the shoulder seams using a narrow French seam, or trim the seam allowance back to 1 cm ($\frac{3}{8}$ in.) and neaten by oversewing the edges together.

When the fabric is gathered, the seamline is treated as a dot and picked up so that the seam lies at the bottom of a tube and remains invisible both while the smocking is being worked and when it is completed.

If the smocked area is to end with a ruffle, a narrow rolled hem is made before drawing up the gathering threads. Two rows of close cable stitch can be worked on the back of the top row to stop the ruffle from rolling forward in wear. Instructions for a bound edge are given on page 132.

2 BASIC TECHNIQUE USING SIMPLE STITCHES

STITCHES

Most smocking stitches have evolved from one basic form of stitch, originally called rope stitch, and now known as outline stitch. Embroiderers will readily recognize this as stem stitch in ordinary surface embroidery. Broadly speaking, the variation in smocking stitches comes from the thread being placed either above or below the needle.

Outline stitch (fig. 27)

As it is a firm stitch and does not stretch too easily, outline stitch is often used as a first row to keep the tubes in place.

Work from left to right. Bring the needle up to the left of the first tube. Pick up the top one-third of the next and each successive tube, keeping the thread below the needle. A second row can be worked close to the first row, but this time keeping the thread above the needle. Two rows worked in this manner can give the appearance of chain stitch.

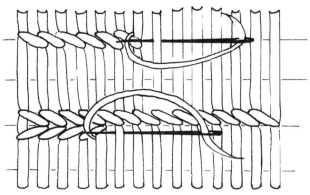

27 *Outline stitch.*

Cable stitch (fig. 28)

This, again, is a firm stitch which can be used to control the tubes at the start of a panel as well as being incorporated into the main design.

Start by bringing the needle up to the left of the first tube. With the thread above the needle, pick up the second tube, inserting the needle from right to left. The third tube is picked up in the same way but with the thread below the needle. Continue across the row in this manner with the thread alternately above and below the needle.

Double cable stitch (fig. 28)

For this, work two rows of cable stitch touching each other. The upper-thread stitch of the second row is placed against the lower-thread of the first row. The result resembles the links of a chain.

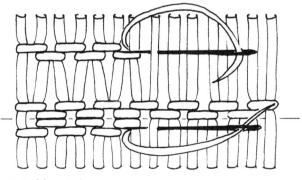

28 *Cable stitch.*

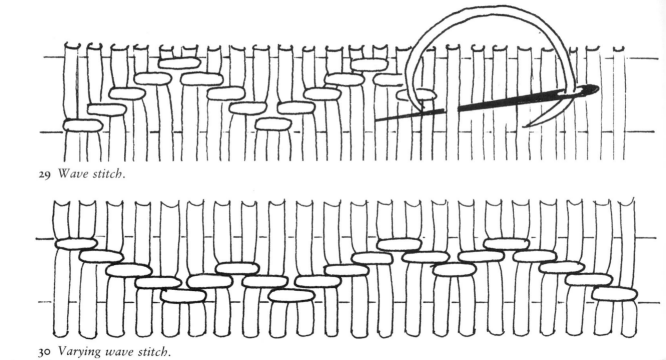

29 *Wave stitch.*

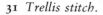

30 *Varying wave stitch.*

Wave stitch (fig. 29)

This stitch is worked on the diagonal between two rows of gathering threads; it is worked on the same principle as cable and outline stitches. It is easier to master wave stitch and keep a smooth line if an uneven number of stitches are worked up and down each wave. With your eye, divide the area between two gathering threads into quarter, half and three-quarter steps. Working down the gathers, bring the needle up to the left of the first tube on a gathering thread. Keeping the thread above the needle, pick up the second tube with the needle straight and the stitch level with the gathering thread. Take a stitch into the third tube at the quarter step, again with the needle straight and the thread above the needle. Take two more stitches in the same way into the

fourth and fifth tubes (half and three-quarter steps), and finally into the sixth tube on the gathering line. Remember to keep the thread above the needle in each case. This completes the downward slope.

For the upward slope, take a stitch in the seventh tube on the same level as the last stitch, with the needle straight and the thread below the needle. Progress upwards, keeping the thread below the needle. Each stitch taken must correspond to the one taken on the downward slope. When working across the row the downward slope may not look as smooth and tidy as the upward slope. If this is the case, make a conscious effort to slant the needle very slightly downwards and this should help. Once the sequence is mastered, the number of stitches used can vary according to the size of wave

31 *Trellis stitch.*

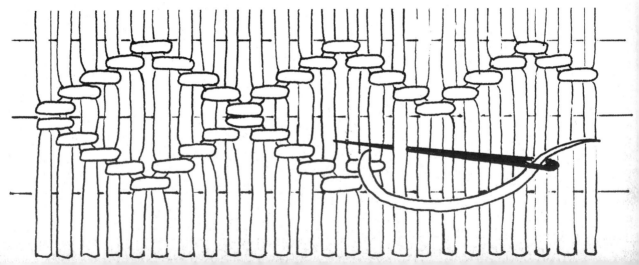

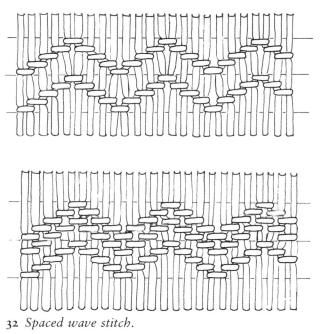

required, and can end halfway between gathering threads or one or two gathering threads above or below the one on which the row started (fig. 30).

Trellis stitch (fig. 31)

This very effective and popular stitch can be used on its own or as a background for further embellishment. It is formed by working a row of wave stitch which is then reversed on the second row to form a diamond shape. Repeated rows will give a trellis effect.

32 *Spaced wave stitch*.

33 *Random spaced wave stitch on silk.*
(Mary Fortune)

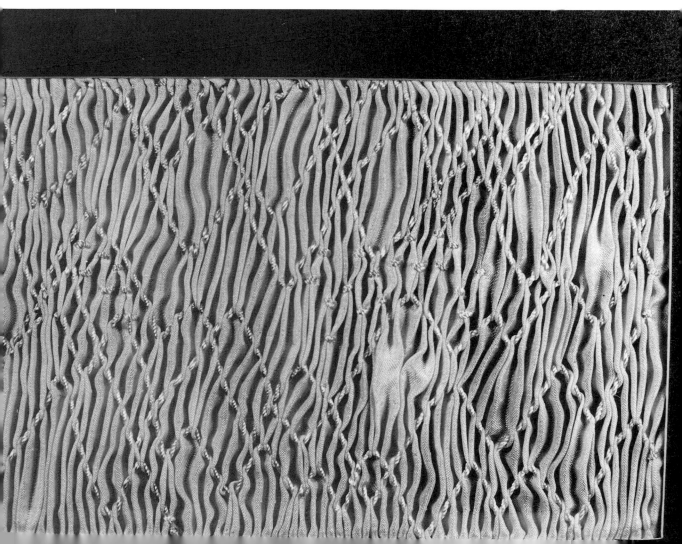

Diamond stitch (fig. 34)

This stitch is worked from left to right between two gathering threads. Bring the needle out on the left of the first tube level with the second row of gathering threads; with the thread below the needle pick up the second tube. Take the thread up to the first row of gathers to pick up the third tube; with the thread above the needle pick up the fourth tube, then with the thread still above the needle go back down to the second row of gathers to pick up the fifth tube. Continue in this way to the end of the row.

This is a zigzag stitch and when worked as a single row gives a loose effect which stretches well. A smaller stitch can be made by working to halfway between the gathering threads.

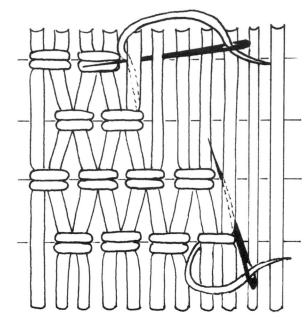

35 *Honeycomb stitch.*

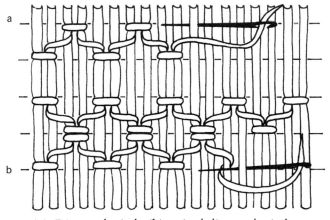

34(a) *Diamond stitch;* (b) *paired diamond stitch.*

Paired diamond stitch (fig. 34b)

This is worked in the same way as the single diamond, with the upper and lower stitches paired off to form a diamond pattern. When a number of rows of diamond stitch are worked in a block, an interesting trellis design is created which has the appearance of spread-out honeycomb. The central tubes can be further embellished with satin stitch or bullion knots.

Honeycomb stitch (fig. 35)

This stitch is very elastic, and most effective when worked in deep panels where the actual stitchery is not required to show too much on the surface. The tubes are drawn into a honeycomb effect, and as so little of the actual stitchery is seen, this stitch is very versatile. A purely textured appearance can be created when the stitch is worked in a matching thread.

It is worked from left to right. Start by coming up

to the left of the first tube in line with the upper gathering thread. Take a stitch through the second and first tubes with the needle straight, then catch them together with a second stitch, this time slipping the needle down the back of the second tube until the second gathering thread is reached. Bring it out to the left-hand side of the tube. Catch the second and third tubes together with a level stitch, take a second stitch over the tubes and slip the needle up the back of the third tube to the level of the upper gathering thread. Continue working up and down across the row. The following row is worked in exactly the same way over the next pair of gathering threads, with the stitches lying on the surface of the tubes like beads.

Surface honeycomb stitch (figs 36 and 37)

This stitch has the high elasticity of honeycomb stitch but can be accomplished a little more easily. It has a very textured quality owing to the thread appearing on the surface of the tubes.

Work from left to right. Start by bringing the needle out on the top row of gathering, to the left of the first tube. With the thread above the needle, pick up the second tube on the same level, inserting the needle from right to left. Keeping the thread above the needle, take a horizontal stitch with the needle going from right to left into the same pleat, but this time on the lower gathering thread. Next, with the thread below the needle, take a horizontal

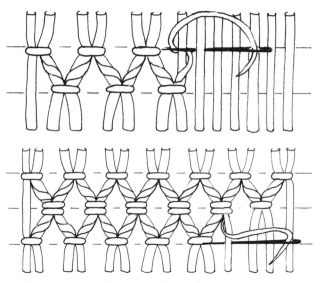

36 & 37 *Surface honeycomb stitch.*

stitch into the third tube on the lower level; still keeping the thread below, insert the needle horizontally through the same tube up at the top level.

For the second row work in the same direction, beginning at the first tube on a lower level and pairing with the first row. The stitch forms diamond shapes similar to diamond stitch, except that there are no tubes left free in the centre of the diamonds. Surface honeycomb is an attractive and extremely versatile stitch.

Vandyke stitch (fig. 38)
This is worked from right to left and is similar in effect to surface honeycomb, except that the stitch is of a squarer appearance. Two tubes are picked up with each stitch and are worked over twice, which makes it a strong stitch whilst giving plenty of elasticity. (However, it is not an easy stitch to undo in the event of an error!)

Start by bringing the needle up to the left of the second tube from the right-hand side, level with the upper gathering thread. Work a horizontal back stitch over the first two tubes. Next, go down to the second gathering thread, insert the needle horizontally through the second and third tubes together, and make a back stitch over them. Go back up to the first gathering thread and work as before over the third and fourth tubes. Continue in this way to the left-hand side of the work. A second row is worked in exactly the same way, but starting so that the top stitch pairs with the lower stitch of the top row.

Feather stitch (fig. 39)
This stitch is worked from right to left and is easier to do if the fabric is turned so as to work back towards yourself. Working between two rows of gathers, pick up two tubes with each stitch. The stitches need to be uniform in size with a very even tension. A little extra practice is often necessary for this stitch.

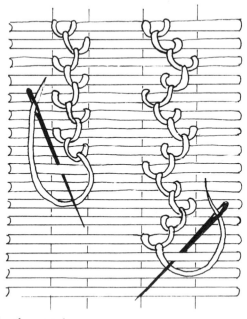

39 *Feather stitch.*

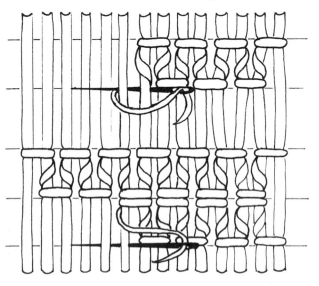

38 *Vandyke stitch.*

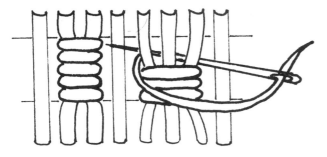

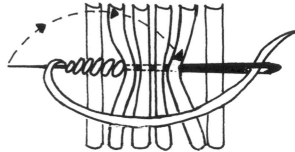

40 *Satin stitch.*

41 *Bullion knot.*

Satin stitch (fig. 40)

This is a particularly useful stitch for adding an extra touch of colour or weight to a 'thin' design. Start by bringing the needle up at the left-hand side of a tube and, taking between two and four tubes together, continue to make horizontal stitches one above the other until the desired space is filled.

Bullion knot (fig. 41)

This stitch can be worked singly or in groups. Three or four bullion stitches worked together will make attractive rosebuds with small detached chain stitches added as leaves. Quite a lot of practice and patience are needed to master this stitch, but the result can be well worth while. Working over four tubes (the number of tubes can vary according to the size of bullion stitch required), bring the needle out on the left-hand side of the first left-hand tube. Then insert it horizontally four gathers to the right

42 *Satin stitch worked over two tubes in the centre of a double diamond stitch can give the feeling of ribbon being woven through the smocking. Cable, wave, diamond, surface honeycomb stitch and small flowerettes are also used within the design.*

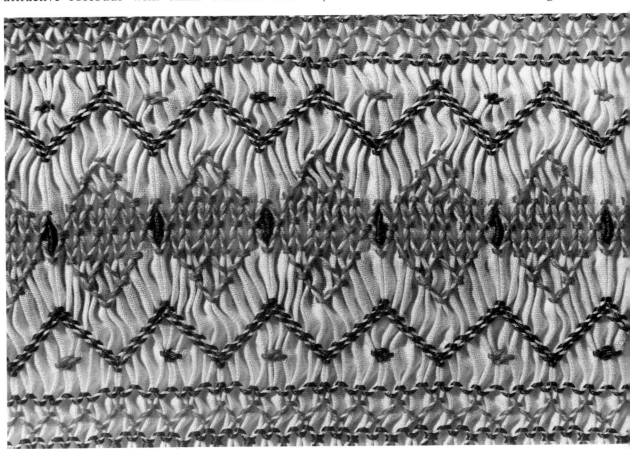

to form a back stitch, bringing the needle point out in the left-hand gather where it first emerged. Do not pull the needle right through the fabric. Twist the thread round the thick part of the needle close to where it emerges from the material. Seven or eight twists are about the number needed to equal the length of the back stitch, but this should be varied according to the thickness of material and thread being used. Still holding the coiled thread, turn the needle back to where it was inserted in the side of the right-hand tube and push it to the wrong side at the same place. Pull the thread through until the bullion stitch lies flat. It should resemble a tiny curved caterpillar on the surface of the fabric.

If the coil becomes loose or tangled whilst the thread is being pulled through, a few strokes with the needle between the twists and the thread will smooth it out.

Small flowerette (fig. 43)

Flowerettes can be particularly effective when worked in the middle of a trellis or used for adding small areas of colour to give impact to a design. Small detached groups of cable stitch are used to make up the flowerettes, with each motif being worked over four tubes. Start by working three cable stitches with the thread alternately below and above the needle, then from the end of the third stitch bring the needle back out to the right of the third tube below the last stitch, and take a level

stitch to the left of the second tube with the thread below the needle. This stitch should nestle comfortably below the previous three to complete the flowerette. Finally, fasten off neatly at the back.

Threads can run up and down inside the tubes, but they should not run across the tubes at the back. It is best to finish off the threads on each individual motif unless they are being worked close together. Threads running across the back can easily get caught up or, more seriously, alter the elasticity and shape of the work.

Large flowerette (fig. 44)

This is formed by means of a small individual trellis pattern worked over six tubes. Starting at the left, come up to the left of the first tube and, keeping the thread below the needle, pick up the second tube on the same level with the needle straight. Take a stitch into the third tube a little higher than the previous stitch, with the thread below the needle. Take a horizontal stitch into the fourth tube to form the top of the trellis with the thread above the needle. With the thread still above the needle, take a stitch a little lower down into the fifth tube. A horizontal stitch on the same level in the sixth tube completes the top half of the trellis. Turn the work upside down to complete the lower trellis and so form the flowerette.

44 *Large flowerette.*

To fill the centre, take two straight stitches one above the other over the two central tubes, using a different colour or tone. Small surrounding leaves can be worked by taking detached chain stitches over two tubes.

STARTING A THREAD

Smocking stitches are worked on the right side of the fabric, with the stitches being started on the left-hand side of the piece except for vandyke and feather stitch. Always start smocking on the second

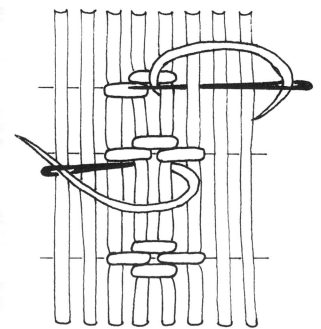

43 *Small flowerette.*

row of gathers; the first row tends to be untidy and can be used as the stitching line when making up the article. The top one-third of the tube is taken with each stitch. Cut a length of thread approximately 45 cm (18 in.) long. A longer thread is liable to tangle and become worn and frayed towards the end. Make a knot in the thread and start by bringing the needle up to the left-hand side of the first tube approximately one-third of the way down. Pull the thread through and continue with the chosen stitch. When using an open or more loosely woven fabric such as voile where the knot could pull through, turn the work to the wrong side and make a small back stitch into the end fold on the gathering line to be smocked. Take the needle back across the fold and push it through to the right side of the fabric where it will emerge on the left-hand side of the first tube.

FINISHING OFF A THREAD

To finish a row, push the needle back down between the tubes where it emerged on completion of the last stitch. Take two or three small back stitches into the bottom of the tube on the wrong side. If a thread is not long enough to complete a row, push the needle through to the back and finish off with two or three tiny stitches. Start the new thread with a knot, and in order to keep the stitches continuous, bring the needle back out where the previous thread has gone down. The same method is used if different coloured threads are being introduced into a pattern.

USEFUL TIPS

- It is possible to keep the *edges* of the smocking neat and tidy by following the method already described for starting and finishing a row of stitching. If, however, the ends of the rows appear at all uneven or the stitch pattern has not ended quite as it should, this can be corrected by means of small pin tucks worked by hand on the wrong side, close to the edge of the smocking. These pin tucks give a very neat finish and help to 'frame' the work. Rows of feather stitch, herring-bone stitch, french knots or other suitable surface embroidery stitch can give an attractive and textural finish when worked close to the smocked edge.

- When smocking is to be used for *fashion*, it is worked before the garment is made up. Before gathering the fabric, oversew the edges, giving generous seam allowances to avoid fraying and distortion caused by excessive handling. The seams are trimmed to size during the actual making-up.

- If the smocking is to end where *extra elasticity* is essential, such as at the waistline, sleeve edge or top of a sundress, a piece of narrow elastic can be attached, using herringbone stitch, on the wrong side across the bottom or top of the smocking. This will hold the stitching and prevent over-stretching through constant wear. In places where texture rather than elasticity is required, such as on a yoke or shoulder strap, a fine lining cut to the correct size and shape may be used.

- It is helpful, when embroidering two *identical panels*, such as collars, cuffs or bodice fronts, to work them together, stage by stage, as any minor design changes can then be repeated immediately.

- Working row by row across a *very wide piece* can appear endless. It is more interesting and far less daunting to thread a number of needles, work a little of each row and gradually progress across the whole design. By working small areas at a time it is also easy to make any minor stitch or colour adjustments which may be found necessary.

- When there are areas within a design, such as the large diamond shape on the dress front illustrated in figure 81, which are to be *left unsmocked*, there is a chance that the tubes may flatten or distort. To prevent this, work a row of cable stitch on the back of the tubes to hold them in place.

- Smocking used in conjunction with an area of *flat fabric*, such as on a dress, bag or cushion, may need a 'finishing touch' of some description to give a balance or framework to the whole design. This can be achieved in a number of ways. Lace, ribbons, french knots, beads, surface stitchery or piping can all help to give added impact and complete the concept.

45 *Egg cosy. Tones of cream and brown silk buttonhole twist worked over polyester/cotton with hand-twisted silk cord couched around the edge.* (Dora Baker)

FINISHING TOUCHES

When all the smocking has been completed and before removing the gathering threads, place a damp cloth over the area and carefully hold a hot iron slightly above it to create steam. Alternatively, a steam iron and a dry cloth can be used. Do not allow the iron actually to touch the smocking, as this could flatten and distort the work. Once the panel is cool and dry and ready to be set into a yoke or similar area, remove all but the top gathering thread, as this is to be used as the seam line. Proceed with making up the article. Both the top and bottom gathering threads are left in when the smocking is to be used as an insertion. If the panel is not being set into an area and a join is unnecessary, all the threads should be removed at this stage.

STRETCHING

When a piece of smocking appears to be too tight to fit into a given area, it is possible to stretch it slightly without causing distortion. To do this, leave in the top and bottom gathering threads; gently pull to the required size and shape and pin on to an ironing board or similar surface. Carefully steam the area, making sure it is completely dry and cool before unpinning or moving it in any way. Once the stretching and steaming process has been followed, the panel will retain its new sizing.

WASHING AND CARE OF SMOCKING

Smocking is remarkably hardwearing and will retain its shape and elasticity through constant washing. Articles can be hand or machine washed using a suitable washing powder at a temperature and setting recommended for the fabric and threads. Do not scrub the smocked area, as this could distort the tubes and impair the embroidery. Drip dry the article and then iron up to the gathered area, but not over it. The smocking should not require any further attention other than pulling into shape. If any tubes have become distorted or flattened, the area can be pinned into shape and lightly steamed.

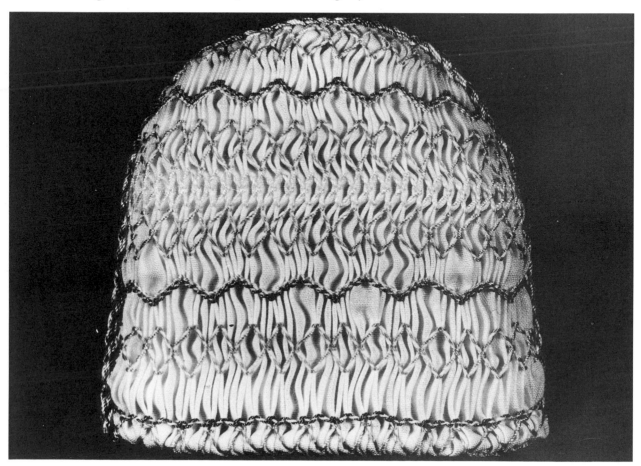

3 WIDENING THE SCOPE

It is very difficult to lay down hard and fast rules in smocking which can guarantee an exact effect. Guidelines can be given, the technique explained and suggestions made for obtaining highly satisfactory results. However, a great deal depends on individual interpretation as well as the individual method of working. Not everyone produces the same stitch or design to look exactly the same, although each is correct and equally valid. Even the same worker can find that results vary from piece to piece. What is stunning one time may well be disappointing the next, owing to a different choice of fabric, thread or colouring. A stitch design worked on a small scale between gathering threads a quarter of an inch (or half a centimetre) apart will be much firmer and more compact than the identical design worked with the gathering threads half an inch (or roughly a centimetre) apart, even if the fabric and threads are the same. All this suggests that time spent working a sampler is never wasted.

46 A sampler showing cable, diamond and vandyke stitch used as the centre for a log cabin patchwork cushion. (Mary Welton)

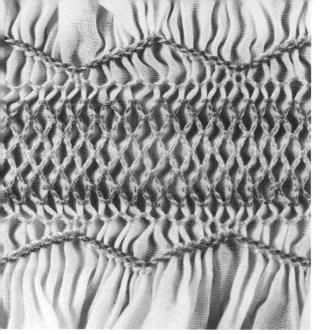

47 *Four tones of pink silk buttonhole twist worked on polyester/cotton make an attractive detachable frill. This design, which is made up of wave stitch, cable stitch and surface honeycomb stitch, is very elastic.* (Jean Hodges)

48 *Surface honeycomb stitch over white binca canvas. The highly textured effect is emphasized when turned so that the tubes run horizontally. This would be most exciting incorporated into sports wear.* (Mary Fortune)

SAMPLERS

A sampler is a practice piece and should be used to learn in the first instance how to work the stitches, then how to develop them, and finally to try out designs and colour schemes before embarking on a finished project. They should be kept as a means of reference, much as one would keep a notebook.

To invent a completely 'new' stitch may appear difficult, if not impossible, but it is surprising how many unconscious variations on an existing stitch can be created by misunderstanding or misinterpreting an instruction and placing either the needle or the thread in a slightly different position. These 'mistakes' should never be discarded. Whilst they may not be an accurate interpretation of a specific stitch, their effectiveness could become equally valid. Even if there is no particular use for them at the time of working the sampler, they certainly could be useful on a future occasion when a special effect or design is being sought.

STITCH VARIATIONS

Having learned the basic stitch techniques, it is well worth considering not only other ways in which the stitches can be used, but also how the scale of each stitch can be altered to increase its effectiveness. A few suggestions at this stage may provide a basis for many creative ideas.

Honeycomb stitch (fig. 48)
The beauty and textural quality of honeycomb and surface honeycomb stitch are never out of place, no matter how or where the stitch is used. A panel of surface honeycomb stitch worked to a small scale for the front of a child's dress is extremely practical in view of its high elasticity and is, of course, very decorative. The same stitch worked to a larger scale on a heavier fabric can become far more dramatic. There are many ways to emphasize its sheer simplicity but perhaps the most effective is by working over deep tubes. The impact produced by the play of light upon the deeper tubes and the shadows created will very quickly become apparent.

Honeycomb or surface honeycomb stitch worked boldly on a heavy satin, where elasticity is not of paramount importance, causes the contours of the tubes to become plump and rounded. The same scale used on a binca canvas or similar fabric

37

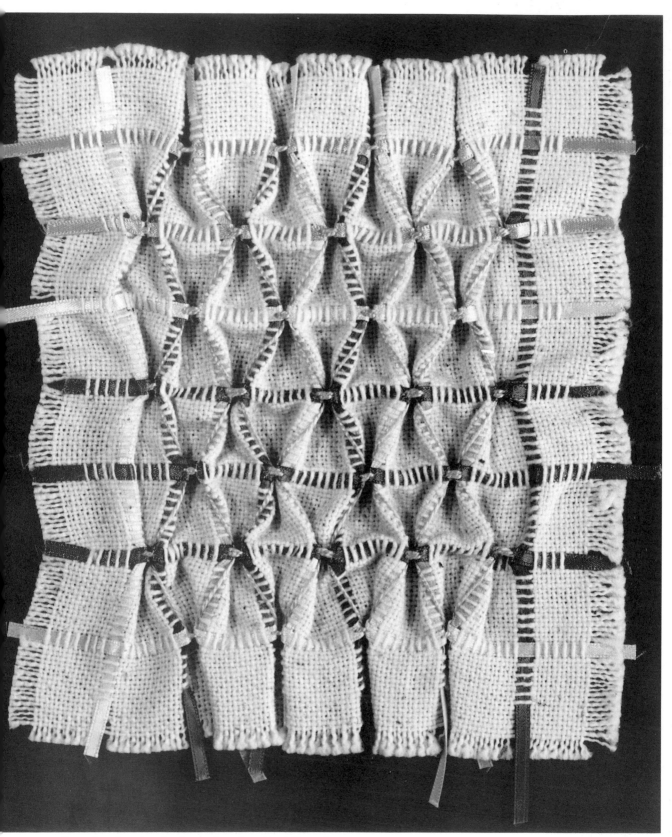

49 *Sampler showing horizontal and vertical threads removed at regular intervals. Narrow ribbons have been threaded through and then smocked, using honeycomb stitch.* (Mary Fortune)

will display a scrunchy, tactile quality (fig. 48). These qualities can be further enhanced by turning the finished work so that the tubes run horizontally instead of vertically, thus allowing the light to catch the tubes and so intensify the shadows they create (see page 57).

A fabric where threads can easily be removed, such as linen, evenweave or folkweave-type furnishing fabric can have them withdrawn vertically, horizontally or both. This can be done at regular or irregular intervals, depending on the effect required. The withdrawn areas can then simply be left as they are or have contrasting threads and ribbons woven through before smocking (fig. 49). The ends of the added threads or ribbons can be secured, or left hanging to give added movement and emphasis. This idea could be particularly effective on the yoke of a jacket, cuffs, bags, cushions or panels.

Cable stitch

An interesting variation of cable stitch can be achieved by dropping a stitch to a lower line, then returning to continue along the line already started. On the next row, drop a stitch either side of the one previously dropped. Continue working in this manner, and a pyramid shape will gradually form (fig. 50). Beads can be added to the thread as it lies between the rows to give extra sparkle and impact. This idea could be developed in many exciting ways for use on garments, bags, boxes or decorative panels.

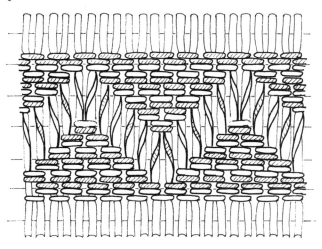

50 *Dropped cable stitch.*

Grouping different numbers of tubes together with individual stitches is another way of introducing interesting variations.

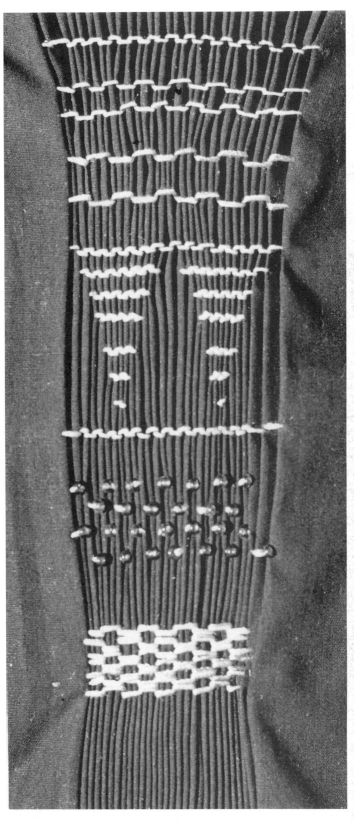

51 *Sampler showing cable stitch variations.* (Sheila Jolly)

39

Zigzag cable stitch (fig. 52)

In order to show this stitch to the best advantage, two colours or types of thread should be used. Start by working a base row of cable stitch in the main colour, then work three cable stitches on alternate sides of the row, using the contrasting colour or thread (fig. 52).

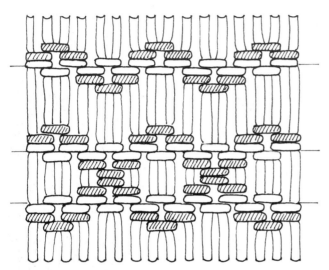

52 Zigzag cable stitch worked in two colours.

Wave stitch variations (figs 53 and 54)

A half-space wave followed by a full-space wave, then again by a half-space wave, will form a diagonal pattern (fig. 53). Working diagonally across a piece enables more colours or tones to be incorporated, as they will appear to merge whereas if used horizontally they remain distinct.

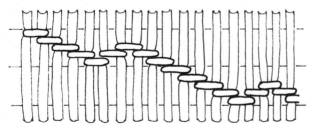

53 Diagonal wave stitch.

When working trellises, interesting variations can be devised by varying the number of tubes used on each or alternate trellises (fig. 54).

Wave stitch can also be made to travel in different directions by turning the work upside down, thus creating a pattern build-up.

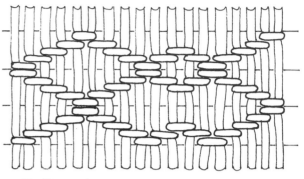

54 Trellis stitch variation.

Vandyke stitch variations (fig. 55)

Vandyke stitch can be worked diagonally in a similar manner to that suggested for wave stitch, giving a more spiky effect. It can also be used in straight diagonal lines to form interesting pointed shapes.

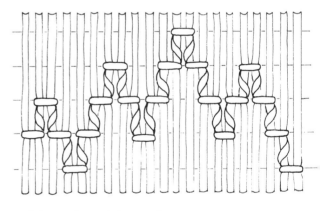

55 Diagonal vandyke stitch variation.

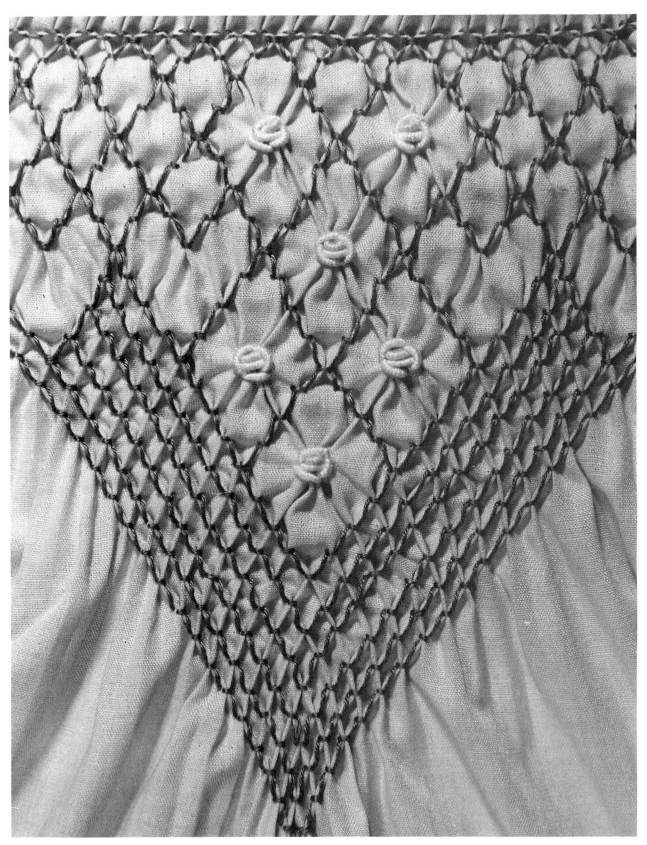

56 *Diagonally worked vandyke stitch forms a firm yet versatile design. The bullion knot rosebuds pull the tubes into interesting shapes.* (Jean Hodges)

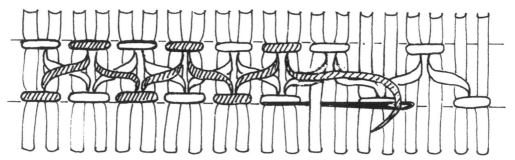

57 *Crossover diamond stitch.*

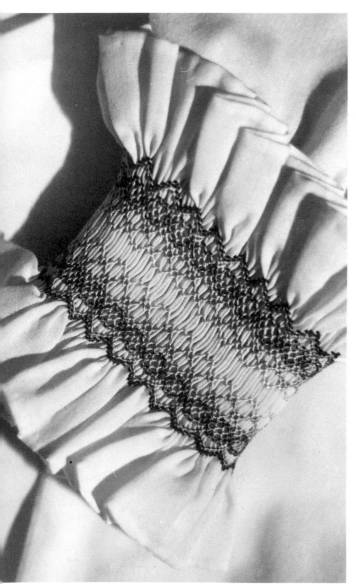

58 *A detachable frill worked in four tones of blue coton à broder on white polyester/cotton. The crossover design of diamond and cable stitch allows the colours to blend more gradually.* (Jean Hodges)

Crossover diamond stitch (fig. 57)

Working stitches so that they cross over each other can be a very useful device for subtly blending colours. Embroider one row of diamond stitch. Work a second row in a different colour over the first one by taking together the tubes missed in the first row. Because the 'crossing' stitch does not have to be the same size as that already worked, this technique gives the opportunity for greater flexibility of design.

Where a block of crossover diamond stitch is to be used, the effect can be made more subtle if one or two rows of diamond stitch are worked before introducing the crossing stitch. In this way the colour change can be more gradual and therefore more effective.

There is a tendency for the work to be less elastic when the 'cross-over' idea is included, so check this on a sampler first.

59 *Cable stitch and diamond stitch variations.*

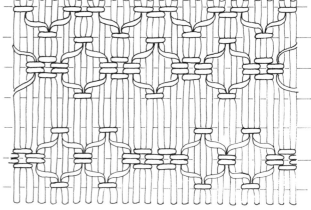

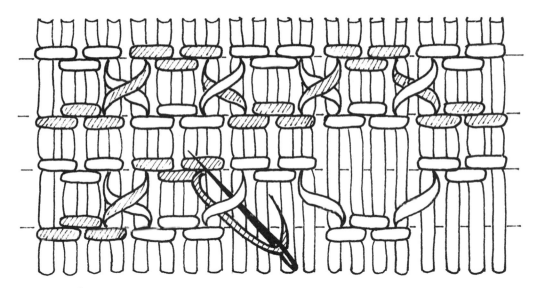

60 *'Weaving' two colours.*

Weaving stitches

In order to obtain even greater versatility, it is possible to 'weave' stitches as well as crossing them over each other. As will be seen in figure 60, the darker thread is taken over the light thread on the 'up' part of the diamond stitch and then woven under on the 'down' stitch. To avoid catching the thread when weaving, turn the needle so that the eye passes under the thread first (fig. 60).

Triple honeycomb stitch (fig. 61)

This is an interesting variation on honeycomb stitch, especially when worked on heavier fabrics with a deep tube. The free tube running through the honeycomb shape gives an added feeling of movement to this highly textural stitch.

Working from left to right, come up to the left of the first tube in line with the upper gathering thread. Take a stitch through the third, second and first tube with the needle straight, then catch them together with a second stitch, this time slipping the needle down the back of the third tube until the second gathering thread is reached. Catch the fifth, fourth and third tubes together with a level stitch, take a second stitch over the three tubes, and slip the needle up the back of the fifth tube to the level of the upper gathering thread. Continue working up and down across the row. The following row is worked in a similar manner over the next pair of gathering threads. It should be noted that the central tube runs free in each group of stitches and the same tube continues down the centre of every row.

Triple surface honeycomb stitch (fig. 62)

This stitch, which is another highly textural and interesting variation on a basic stitch, is formed in a slightly different way from the usual surface honeycomb stitch, in that a second stitch has to be taken each time to secure the free central tube.

Work from left to right. Start by bringing the needle out on the top row of gathering to the left of

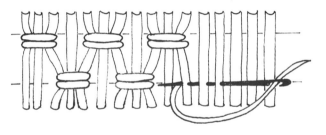

61 *Triple honeycomb stitch.*

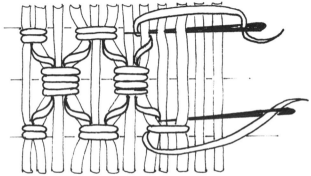

62 *Triple surface honeycomb stitch.*

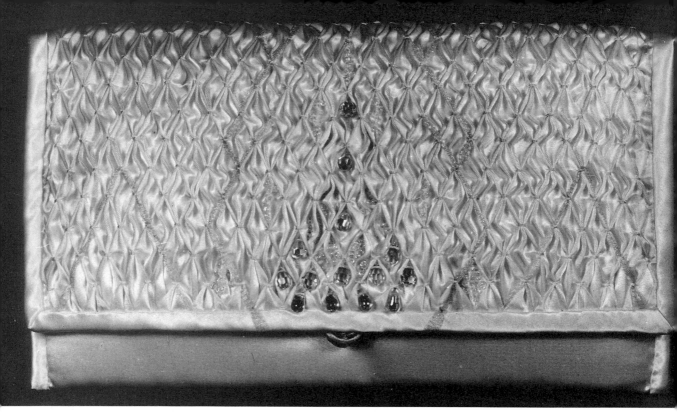

63 *White satin evening bag worked in triple honeycomb stitch. Crystal beads have been added in the cells. (Jean Hodges)*

64 *Detail of fig. 63.*

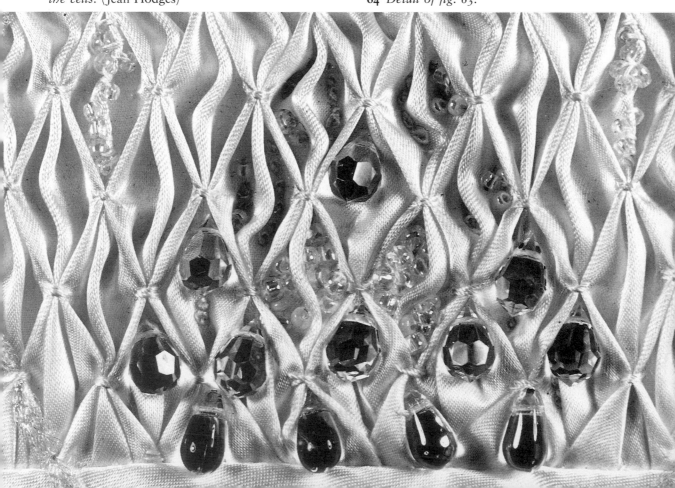

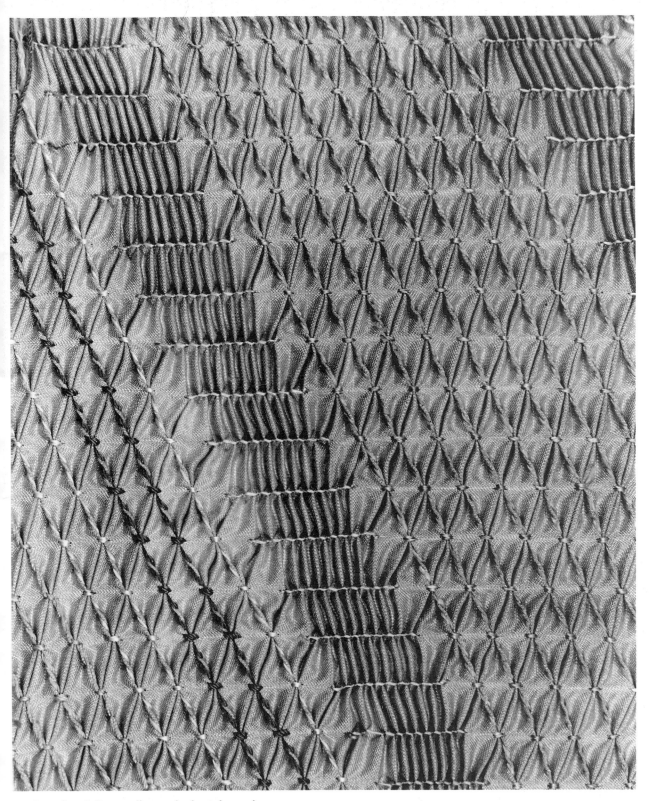

65 *Sample of diagonally worked triple surface honeycomb stitch and outline stitch worked on random-dyed silk.* (Gillian Jenkins)

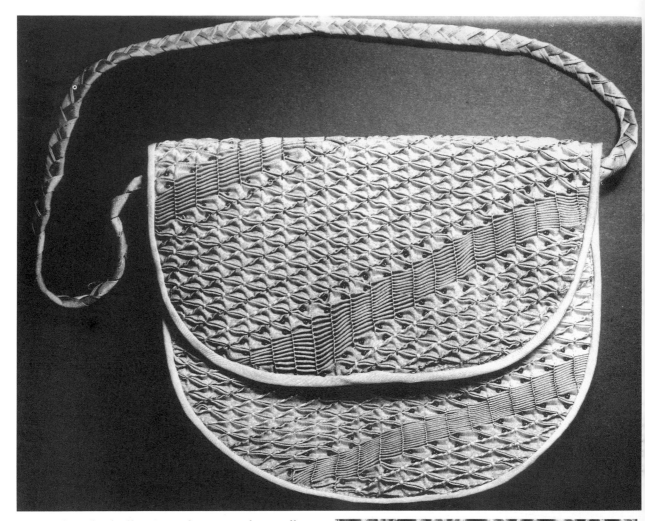

66 *Random-dyed silk evening bag using diagonally worked triple surface honeycomb stitch and outline stitch, with added beads to give a textured appearance.* (Gillian Jenkins)

67 *Detail of a cushion centre. Triple surface honeycomb stitch worked in a diamond pattern, using synthetic knitting yarn.* (Jean Hodges)

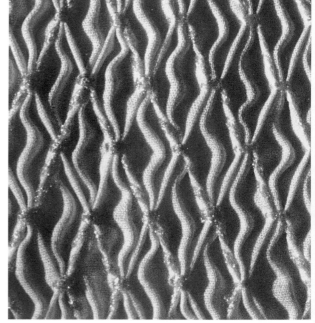

the first tube. With the thread above the needle, take a stitch from right to left through the third, second and first tubes, keeping the needle straight. Take a second stitch over the three tubes, bringing the needle out on the left side of the third tube. With the thread above the needle, take a horizontal stitch with the needle going from right to left into the same (i.e. third) tube on the lower gathering thread. Take a straight stitch from right to left through the fifth, fourth and third tubes. With the thread below the needle, take a second stitch over the three tubes, bringing the needle out to the left of the fifth tube.

Keeping the thread below, insert the needle from right to left through the fifth tube at the upper gathering thread. Continue working up and down across the row, taking in two new tubes each time.

The following row is worked in the same manner, beginning at the first tube on the lower gathering thread and pairing the stitches with the first row.

Diagonally worked triple surface honeycomb stitch can be particularly effective. Its use can add an entirely new dimension to the piece, with the light catching the tubes in a different way and colours blending more easily (see fig. 65).

Baskets (fig. 68)

An attractive flower basket motif, which can be worked either singly or in a row, is created by using double cable stitch. This stitch, when worked in a block, resembles the weaving on a basket. The handle is depicted by satin and stem stitch. Flowers can be added with detached chain stitch, bullion knot rosebuds, french knots, beads or any suitable surface stitches, using textured threads and ribbons for added interest. Instructions are given for a large basket, with a diagram only for the smaller one (fig. 69). These instructions can easily be adapted to suit individual requirements.

The basket is worked over 18 tubes and five gathering threads, although the actual number of

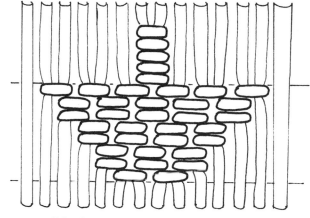

69 *Small basket.*

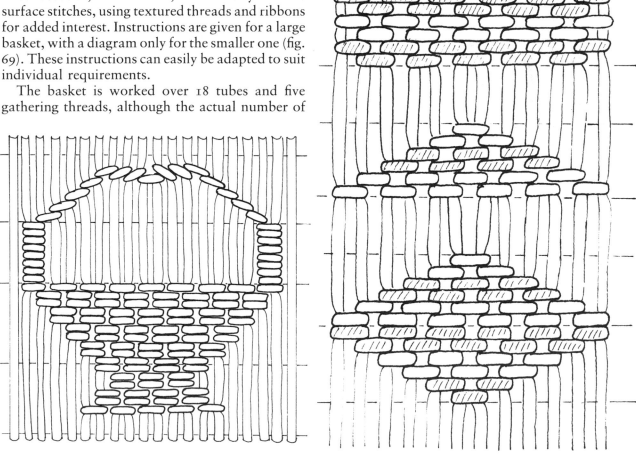

68 *Large basket.*

70 *Cable stitch worked in parallel rows.*

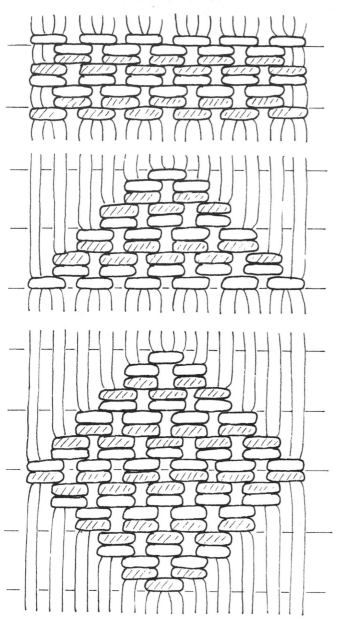

71 *Cable stitch worked in opposite rows.*

basket, work another row of seven stitches and then a final row of nine. The handle is shaped by working satin and stem stitch.

By experimenting with the ways in which stitches are stacked, many pictorial designs and scenes such as houses, trees, vehicles, people and animals can be devised to bring a new and exciting dimension to the work. For example, parallel rows of cable stitch (fig. 70) will produce square shapes, whilst opposite rows will produce pyramids (fig. 71). These free designs can be worked out on graph paper or drawn straight on to the fabric, remembering to pull the gathering threads tight so as to close up the tubes before marking with tailor's chalk. Basic stitches are then used to work the design, adding surface embroidery stitches, ribbons, buttons or beads if required. Blocks of colour can also be created in this manner. When working any block pattern, allow for the possibility of the smocking stretching sideways in use, thus causing slight distortion to the design once the gathering threads have been removed.

THREE-DIMENSIONAL EFFECTS

Owing to the geometric nature of smocking, it is possible to give greater emphasis to the three-dimensional quality by means of a planned use of colour. There is a tendency to think in terms of a single colour being used throughout a row. How-ever, with a few trials, and possibly some errors, surprisingly interesting results can be achieved. For instance, try working two or three rows of closely spaced wave stitch in a dark thread. Using a lighter tone, or perhaps white, work another row with the light colour going close above the first row on the upward slope of the wave, then run the thread down behind the tubes to work a lower row on the downward slope. Continue in this manner, and a pleated three-dimensional ribbon effect will be achieved (fig. 73).

A variety of other shapes can be designed in a similar way, using different colour tones. Ideas should be worked out on graph paper first using coloured pencils or pens, and the time spent can be most rewarding. Ethnic designs, tiles, architecture, photographs, books and magazines can all be valuable design sources.

The flame designs found in Florentine (Bargello) canvas work can also be effectively interpreted into smocking (see colour plate 10). Using wave stitch

gathering threads can vary depending on the depth being used between each row. Starting on the third gathering line, work 17 cable stitches. Continue downwards, using cable stitch, with the upper thread of the lower row against the lower thread of the previous row and working one stitch less at the beginning and end of each successive row until there are seven stitches. The fabric can be turned to enable the stitching to continue backwards and forwards across the rows, rather than starting and stopping at each line. To make the base of the

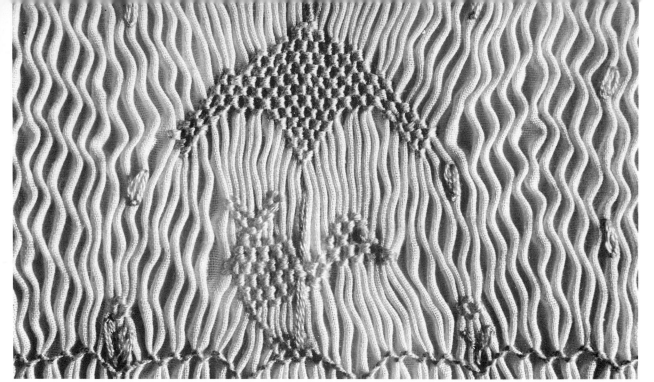

72 'Duck with umbrella' design worked on the front of a child's dress. The background area is held by wave stitch smocking on the reverse. (Heather King)

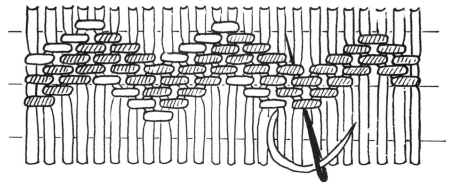

73 Three-dimensional ribbon-effect wave stitch.

with cable stitch where necessary, the rise and fall of the contours can easily be followed, giving beautiful colour blending. This idea would be very suitable for the yoke, sleeve or waistline of a dress, or, alternatively, it could form part of a wall hanging.

It is well worth considering canvas work, cross stitch or knitting charts, many of which can be readily adapted for smocking. Such charts can be particularly successful for working on insertions or where only a narrow band is required.

Altering the size of a stitch within a piece of work is another way of introducing exciting and unusual effects. Fig. 74 shows how surface honeycomb stitch in varying lengths can create an interesting wave design in both the stitching and the background areas. The top row of stitching has a contrasting thread laced through to hold the panel firmly, yet allowing the bottom to fan out freely. This idea would be particularly effective incorporated into fashion, and could look stunning on an evening dress or blouse with glittering threads or beads added in selected areas.

When threads or ribbons are laced through any form of smocking, the natural elasticity of the technique can become restricted. It is advisable, therefore, to check that sufficient allowance is made for the thread or ribbon to stretch the required amount before finally cutting and securing.

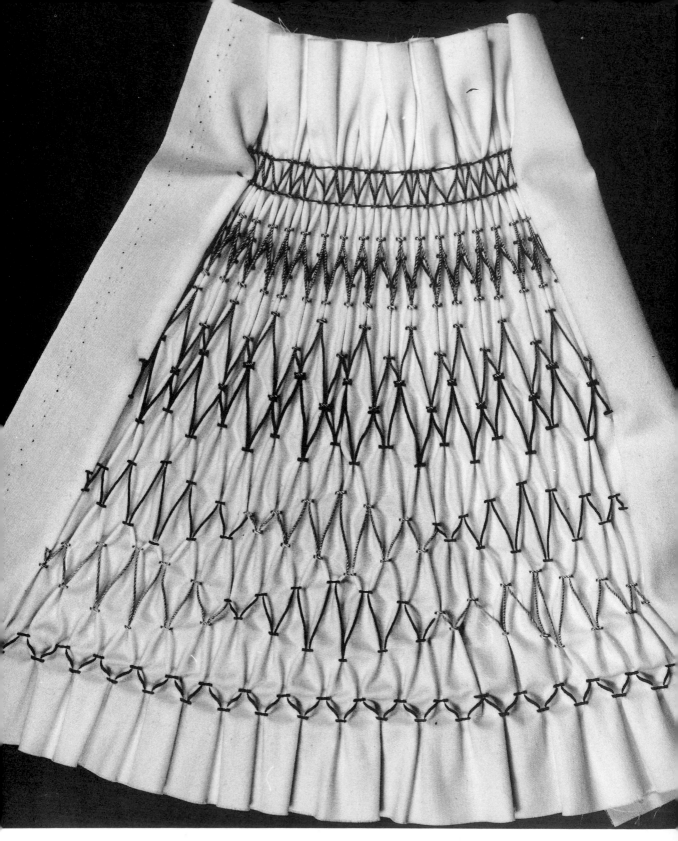

74 *Surface honeycomb stitch. The top row is threaded with a contrasting colour to hold the fabric firmly. By varying the length and colour of the stitch, interesting designs can be built up. (Sheila Jolly)*

4 USING SMOCKED FABRIC

Commercial patterns of any kind which use smocking may be difficult to find in the style or size required, but with careful thought and pre-planning it is possible to adapt many patterns to enable smocking to be included. Instructions for making these adaptations can be found in chapter 7 of *Smocking: Traditional and Modern Approaches* by Œnone Cave and Jean Hodges (Batsford, 1984).

INSERTIONS

Smocked insertions can be an effective yet simple way of adding a decorative or textured panel to an article or garment. The panel may be worked in a contrasting fabric, or in the fabric used for the main article. A contrasting fabric is particularly useful when working in 'difficult' fabrics such as velvet, corduroy, heavy wools or bouclé, where the gathering could cause problems or too much bulk. Any difficulties encountered in choosing a suitable colour for smocking on a patterned fabric can be easily overcome by inserting a smocked panel in a plain fabric, as already described on page 18 (fig. 16). Matt fabrics can be combined with shiny ones, smooth with textured, or light with heavy, to give an imaginative and exclusive finish.

A narrow piping will help to prevent the bulk from the smocking puckering the area around the insertion. Lace, ribbon trim or surface embroidery could also be used to give a neat finish.

Insertions are worked on the straight. They can be used either vertically or horizontally, and are easily manipulated into curves. They can therefore be placed almost anywhere – on a bodice, skirt or sleeve of a dress, or alternatively incorporated into a panel or cushion. A piece of smocking can even be gently coaxed into a circle for inclusion in a round box, cushion or bag. To do this, make sure the finished piece will be long enough for the circumference of the insert. Use tight stitches at the top of the panel to form the inner curve, with a more open, stretchy design for the outer edge. A separate circle of fabric can be applied at the centre if desired, to overcome the bulky join. French knots, beads or surface stitchery would be other ways of neatening the central area.

CURVED PATTERNS IN SMOCKING

In order to widen the range of design ideas, it is possible to create interesting curved patterns and undulating lines. With the tubes pulled tightly together, the outline of the required curve is drawn on to the right side of the fabric, using tailor's chalk or a very fine pencil. The tension is then loosened slightly and the smocking worked over the drawn lines, using either chain stitch or outline stitch. Chain stitch gives a solid, heavy line, while outline has a finer and more delicate appearance. If outline stitch is used, it is worked in the same direction all around the curve. If the stitch is started with the thread below the needle, it should remain below, and not be changed as when working wave stitch.

It may be necessary to exaggerate the depth of curve to allow for the slight distortion caused when the gathering threads are removed and the smocking stretched. A complete half circle drawn on to the fabric will result in a shallower curve when complete.

Many free and pictorial designs can be created in this manner, as well as a very pretty edging. Three curves worked one above the other will create an interesting swag design (fig. 75). The top curve could be very shallow, almost straight, with each successive curve becoming deeper and more exaggerated. Bullion knot rosebuds or narrow ribbon

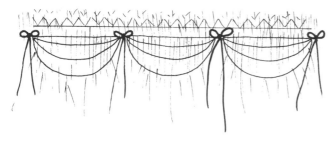

75 *Suggestion for a curved 'swag' design using outline or cable stitch with added ribbons.*

can be placed at the point where the curves join to give added impact. This could look very attractive at the waistline of a dress or at the bottom of a panel for a christening robe.

An optical curve can also be created by working one side of a wave, then five or seven cable stitches on the straight followed by the other side of a wave. This can be effective when worked within a panel or

76 *Cable and wave stitch are stepped to form a curve. Added interest is given by the way in which the cable stitch holds the tubes together. The large area within the curve is held in place by cable stitch on the reverse.* (Jean Hodges)

design where the smocking can be stretched slightly for greater emphasis.

It is also possible to create a larger curved panel by means of steps. Wave stitch down between two or more gathering threads, five cable stitch on the straight, wave stitch down again. Continue working this sequence until the required depth is reached, then return up in the same manner. If a number of rows is to be used, as in fig. 76, an extra stitch can be worked at each end of the bottom cable stitch sequence. This also has the added interest that the tubes form pillars between the rows of cable stitches to give an architectural feel. This idea could be used for free expression; on the front of a dress or blouse or radiating up from the bottom of a sleeve. Cable stitch worked on the back will hold the large area within the curve in place (fig. 77). It is also worth noting how the tubes ripple and bend at the back of the curved area, to such an extent that the piece could be very exciting used the reverse way round.

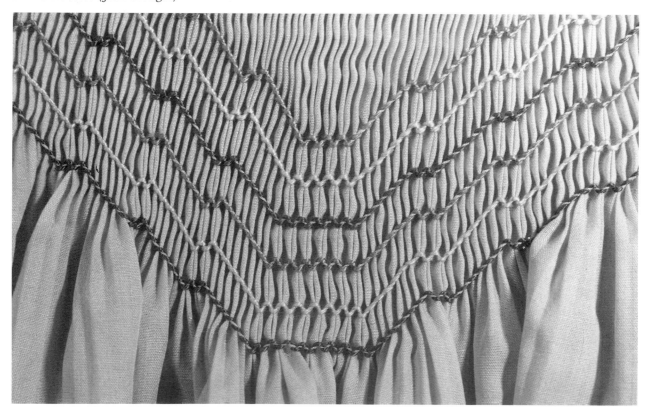

77 *The back of fig. 76, showing how effective the design would be used either way round.*

CUTTING SMOCKING

Greater versatility in the use of smocking can be achieved by regarding a piece of smocked fabric as a piece of material which can be cut to fit a neckline, an armhole or any other shaped area. Of course, it is possible to cut the smocking dots to the required shape before they are gathered, but this can cause certain difficulties, especially in maintaining the flow of the stitch design, and in ensuring a perfect fit. It is much easier and avoids unnecessary distortion if the smocking is worked as a straight panel and then cut to shape.

In preparing for this sort of application, first smock the fabric on the straight of grain to the required depth and width, equivalent to the widest measurement of the pattern piece. Steam the work, stretching it slightly, then remove all but the first and last gathering threads. Pin the smocking out to shape on an ironing board or similar surface. Place the paper pattern on the embroidery, taking care to match the centre of the pattern to the centre tube for its entire length. Make sure that the smocking lines are also aligned with the pattern. A few extra horizontal and vertical straight lines drawn on the paper pattern may be found useful when matching up. Pin in position and loosely tack all around the cutting line (not the stitching line!). Remove the pattern piece and machine stitch, using a narrow zigzag or a straight stitch, just inside the tacked line, so that the stitching actually comes within the seam allowance. The embroidery can then be cut and made up like any other piece of fabric without fear of the work unravelling.

Where smocking is being joined to an unsmocked piece at the shoulder seam, turn both the seam allowances towards the unsmocked area to give a flatter finish.

When a pattern piece needs to be put to a fold in the fabric such as a bodice front, it is advisable to cut a new pattern to cover the whole area. Fold the new pattern in half and pin the bottom layer to the right side of the smocked fabric, ensuring that the fold runs accurately down the centre pleat. The upper shoulder edge should be level with the raw edge. Without moving the pins, unfold the pattern and pin the other half in place. Tack around the neck, shoulder and armhole edges and proceed as already described. Once this method of cutting has been mastered and confidence built up, the machine stitching can be omitted.

For the First Communion dress shown in fig. 79,

three widths of polyester fabric were joined together and the seams pressed open so that they were very flat. It was then gathered on a gathering

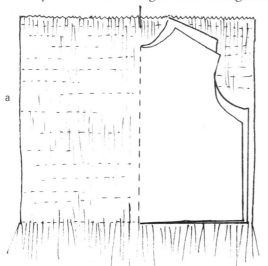

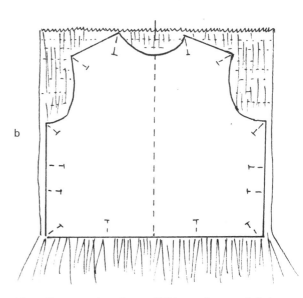

78 (a) *Bottom layer pinned to the right side of the fabric;* (b) *pattern opened out fully and pinned in place.*

79 *First Communion dress. White polyester fabric smocked and cut to shape. (Susan MacNamara)*

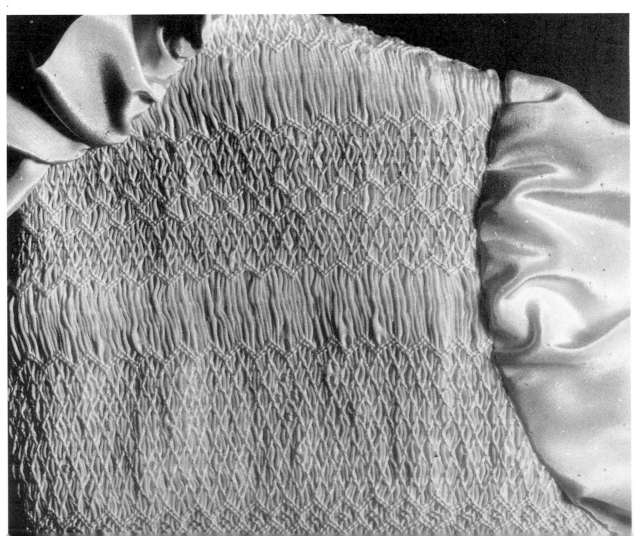

80 *First Communion dress. White polyester smocked in four shades of pink and white coton à broder. The neck and shoulders were cut after being smocked. (Susan MacNamara)*

machine and smocked as a complete panel, using coton à broder. After smocking, all but the top gathering thread were removed. The neck and armhole areas were then cut out following a simple, straightforward dress pattern (not designed to include smocking). A lining was added to give stability at the shoulders and armholes, but left to hang freely at the waistline, thus enabling the smocking to stretch as necessary.

81 *Child's dress. Two widths of cream polyester/ cotton were stitched together and smocked. Tones of pink and brown silk buttonhole twist were used, with panels of crossover diamond stitch at the sides to help blend the colours. The front was then cut out with the tubes running horizontally to give greater interest.* (Jean Hodges)

82 *Shaped bodice front. The cable and wave stitch design was built up from border patterns, with reverse smocking holding the unsmocked tubes in place.* (Helen Waycott)

Fig. 81 shows a child's dress with the smocking cut to fit the shaped front. Two widths of fabric were joined, smocked and cut in such a way that the tubes run horizontally rather than vertically.

HORIZONTAL SMOCKING

Horizontally placed smocking can add yet another dimension which is well worth considering. The simplest of stitch patterns take on a new meaning and the light reflects in a different way – it catches

83 *Pale blue and white cotton fabric smocked in navy blue and white. Piping and broderie anglaise trim, with navy blue thread woven through, completes the design.* (Rose Glennie)

84 *Detail of fig. 83.*

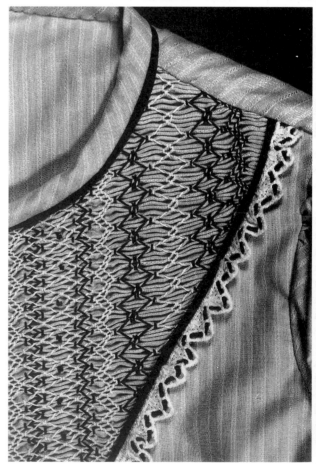

across rather than up and down the gathers. Horizontal smocking also has the added advantage that the tubes are included in the side seams of a garment. This allows complete freedom for any shaping required in the unsmocked area to be added by means of darts or tucks, rather than the usual fullness of gathers.

TEXTURES

There are occasions when added emphasis and richness may be needed, and this can be achieved in a number of different ways. The tubes can be embroidered before the gathers are pulled up to bring out a specific colour or design, surface embroidery or beads can be added after the smocking has been worked, or the actual cells can be filled with beads, sequins or stitchery. Beads can also be threaded on to the needle and attached as the tubes are stitched together, so that they sit on top of the

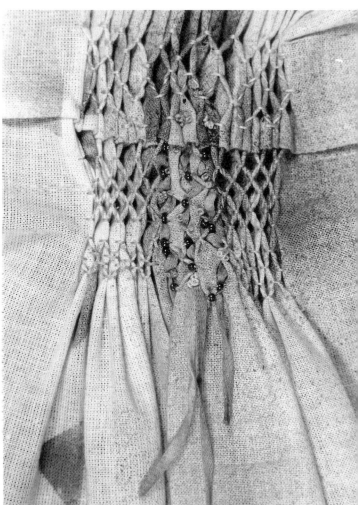

85 *Top picture: surface honeycomb stitch worked in strips of torn fabric; lower picture: vandyke stitch variation.* (Mary Fortune)

86 *Sampler. Horizontal tucks with surface honeycomb stitch and added ribbons, beads and french knots. A light spraying with fabric paint gives a subtle colour variation.* (Valerie Cleveland)

gathers, or they can be threaded so as to hang freely either from the stitchery or in the background cells to give sparkle and movement. Ribbons, leather, cords and cut or torn strips of fabric can be woven through the cells; fine organzas or iridescent fabrics are particularly exciting. The main criterion is that the method chosen should be compatible with the way in which the smocking is to be used.

Slight changes of tone and textural appearance can be achieved by tightening the working thread as it passes from one stitch to another, thus forming a slight pucker or tuck. Honeycomb stitch is particularly suitable for this treatment, although experimentation with different types and sizes of stitch could produce interesting and unusual effects.

Parallel areas of flat fabric left between blocks of

smocking can be an effective way to highlight the textural quality. It is also possible to introduce other techniques within these flat panels by means of pin tucks, hand or machine embroidery, quilting, appliqué, beads, surface stitchery or ribbons. The sample illustrated in figs 87 and 88 is one interpretation of this idea. Two panels of smocking, bound with bias strips, were joined to the central and side panels with an openwork seam. The bias-bound central panel was further embellished by random-spaced pin tucks and areas of feather stitching. The smocking and embroidery were worked in coton à broder on Swiss lawn, with cotton lace trimming. This idea could be developed for an exquisitely delicate christening robe or perhaps used on a

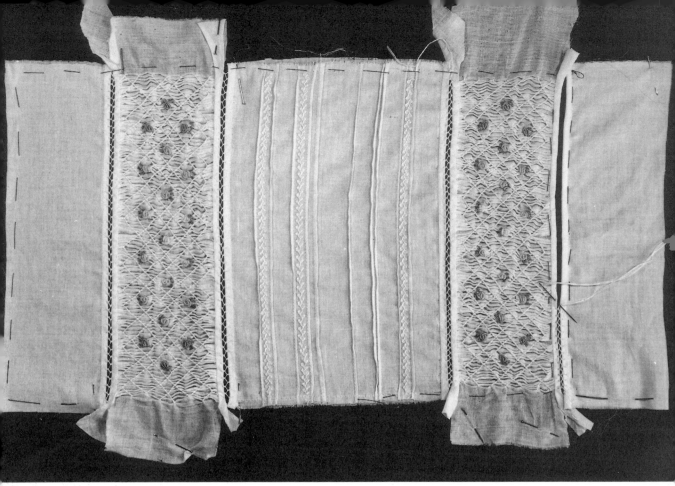

87 Panels joined by means of openwork seams.
Pin tucks and feather stitching have been added for
extra texture. (Jean Hodges)

88 Detail of fig. 87 showing close-up of the seam.
A simple background smocking design has been used,
with bullion knot roses added within the large
squares. (Jean Hodges)

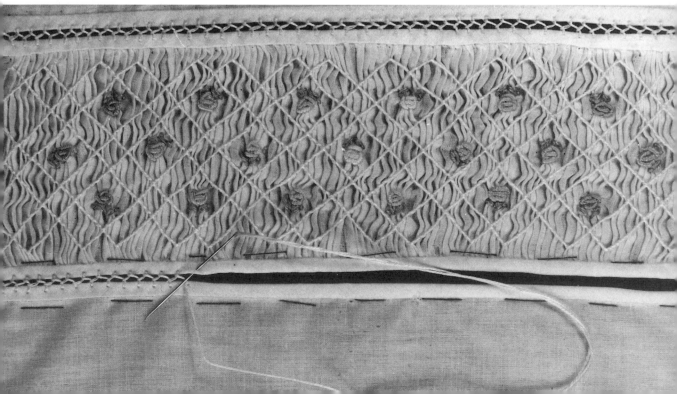

blouse or dress, as well as a cushion or similar article.

Openwork seams may be used to advantage when joining smocking to unsmocked areas. This method could help to overcome any puckering caused by variations in bulk between the pieces being joined, as well as adding a new dimension. Each piece to be joined must have its raw edges finished off with a binding or a narrow hem. The pieces are then joined by means of one of the many attractive insertion stitches. An open, lacy texture is formed with this stitching, through which narrow ribbons could be threaded if more emphasis was needed in a colour scheme. Beads could also be added for extra sparkle.

CREATING STRIPED FABRICS

It is generally assumed that striped fabric for use with smocking, or indeed any other form of embroidery, should be ready-printed or woven. While it can be very convenient to purchase these fabrics, there are other ways of producing a striped effect which have the advantage of giving the right texture and colour for a specific purpose.

One method is illustrated in fig. 89. Strips of random-dyed material and net were machined together, using a small zigzag stitch, to form a striped fabric which was then honeycomb smocked with tapes and thread to give a richness and feeling of depth. The frayed edges of some of the strips add to the misty quality which is created by the blending of colour.

It is also possible to join varying widths of soft ribbon together in a similar manner by hand or machine, using a zigzag or straight stitch. The resulting fabric can then be smocked using honeycomb or triple-honeycomb stitch. Such ideas could be stunning when used in a garment, as suggested in the sketch in fig. 90, or used experimentally for inclusion in panels or wall hangings.

Fig. 91 shows a piece of cotton fabric which was gathered and sprayed with metallic car spray to give a soft, uneven stripe effect. It was then smocked, with varying numbers of tubes being taken together, using random-coloured metallic machine thread and twisted silky threads.

For a more general and hardwearing purpose, stripes can be created by using fabric paints. For this method, narrow widths of masking tape are stuck to the fabric and then the paint is sprayed, painted

89 *Strips of random-dyed fabric and net machined together to form a striped background for smocking.* (Sheila Jolly)

or stippled on to the exposed areas. The tape is removed, and the fabric ironed to fix the paint, or treated according to the manufacturer's instructions. Transfer paints and crayons can also be used, in which case the stripes are put on to paper and then ironed on to the fabric like an ordinary embroidery transfer. A great advantage of any of these methods is your complete freedom to choose the colours, as well as the placing of the stripes, to obtain the desired effect. Stripes can be interspersed within a panel of smocking, worked alongside the smocking, above or below it, or indeed in any direction.

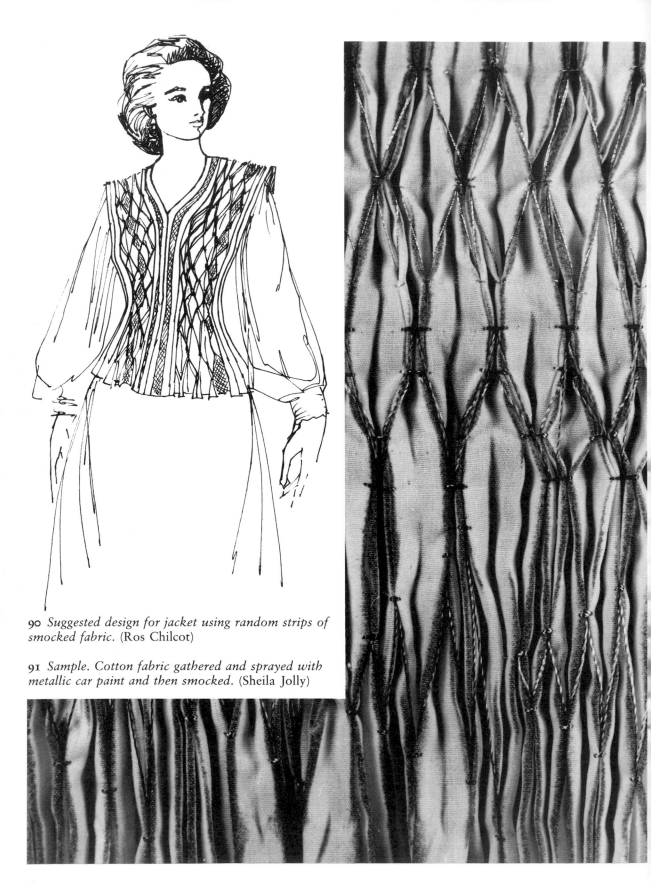

90 *Suggested design for jacket using random strips of smocked fabric.* (Ros Chilcot)

91 *Sample. Cotton fabric gathered and sprayed with metallic car paint and then smocked.* (Sheila Jolly)

RIBBONS

Ribbons of all types and widths can be included to create interesting and exciting effects. They are available in a wide variety of colours, textures and widths, making them extremely versatile. Narrow ribbons can be used to form the actual stitches on a more open fabric. Varying widths can be threaded through the cells from top to bottom, placed in isolated areas, or threaded horizontally and looped through the actual stitches. Ribbons can be gathered, ruched or folded and then applied either vertically or horizontally to a smocked panel. They can be stitched in place using surface embroidery stitches, held down with beads, or the ends can be left hanging freely to give movement and possible colour balance to a design.

White satin ribbon 2 mm ($\frac{1}{16}$ in.) wide has been woven and threaded through a background design of diamond stitch worked on red polyester/cotton to create the Christmas ball decoration in fig. 92.

The design on the yoke of the christening robe in fig. 94 has been highlighted by weaving 6 mm ($\frac{1}{4}$ in.) white satin ribbon through the smocking. 2 mm ($\frac{1}{16}$ in.) white satin ribbon was used to make the french knot rosebuds, with detached chain stitches in pale green coton à broder added to form the leaves. The panel was worked, then cut to shape, mounted on to a lining and the dress made up using a simple dress pattern.

Added impact and textural contrast can be achieved by cutting the fabric and slotting the

92 *'Christmas Ball.' Made from a straight strip of red fabric smocked in white, with narrow ribbons woven through the stitching.* (Heather King)

93 *Ribbon slotted through smocking.*

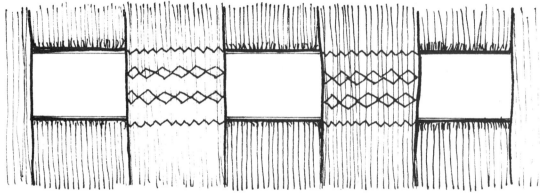

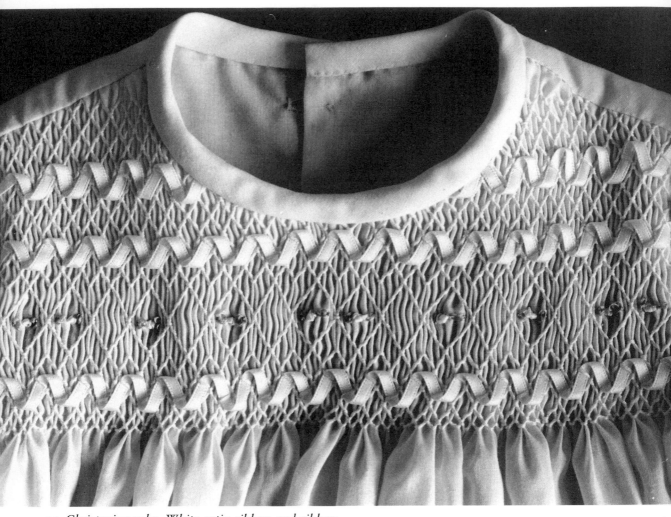

94 *Christening robe. White satin ribbon and ribbon rosebuds highlight the simple background design.* (Heather King)

ribbons behind and in front of smocked areas (fig. 93). To do this, mark the channel between two tubes where the ribbon is to be inserted before starting to smock. The depth to be marked will be the width of the ribbon plus 3 mm ($\frac{1}{8}$ in.). Work the smocking design between the marked tubes, making sure no stitches are carried across the area that is to be cut. Complete the whole panel, steam it and remove all but the top and bottom gathering threads, if they are required for making up. Using small, sharp embroidery scissors, carefully cut the fabric where

marked. Work fine buttonhole stitch by hand around the slit to neaten the edges. This could be a delightful way of adding a belt to the waistline of a dress.

A very attractive cushion or box top could be designed by working a panel of smocking using this method of slotting through ribbons to give a chequerboard effect. The area covered by the ribbon need only be held by smocking on the back. The areas of actual smocking could then be kept quite simple by using a form of honeycomb or diamond stitch, or made more elaborate by working a different stitch in each section, giving a patchwork sampler effect.

1 *A smocked apron with a matching border embroidered in traditional surface stitchery.*
Made by Œnone Cave.

2 *A child's viyella dress smocked in yellow and two shades of blue. The stitches used are outline, feather, cable, wave and surface honeycomb.*
Made by Œnone Cave.

3 Blouse and skirt designed to be used
for folk dancing. The skirt is smocked
into a waistband with an embroidered
belt attached. The yoke of the blouse
and wide border above the hem of the
skirt are embroidered with original
designs of surface stitchery to depict
traditional motifs in a modern idiom.
Made by Œnone Cave for
Sheena Squibbs.

4 A cushion designed to incorporate all
the motifs found during an extensive
research of surviving nineteenth-
century smocks.
Made by Œnone Cave.

5 *Spray painting over triple honeycomb-smocked*
   white satin on the cuffs, yoke insert and
   headdress adds a romantic touch to a simply
   styled wedding dress.
   Made by Jean Hodges for Caroline Dedman.
   (Photo: Mike Farmer)

6 *Detail of Waterfall panel showing surface*
smocking with the addition of hand and machine
embroidery.
Made by Ros Chilcot.

7   *Peasant blouse worked in six tones of silk buttonhole twist on cotton lawn by Jean Hodges for Elizabeth Hodges. (Photo: Mike Farmer)*

8   *The neckline of this polyester/cotton baby dress is cut on the straight of the grain with smocking used to create the curve. Bullion knot rosebuds give an attractive finish to the simple design. Made by Joy Hopkyn-Rees.*

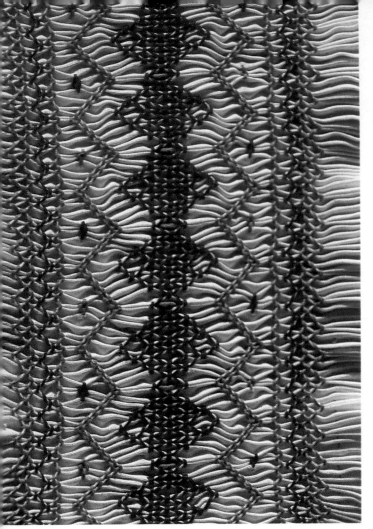

9   Here Jean Hodges has used cable, diamond and wave stitch with small flowerettes for extra impact. 'The horizontally placed tubes help to catch the light.'

10   A combination of reverse smocking, quilting and hand stitching have been used on these panne velvet, three-dimensional pigeons. Made by Jill Friend.

11 *French knots and beads nestle into a*
background of reverse smocking to form the
base of a richly decorated silk box.
From the Embroiderers' Guild Collection.

12 *Smocked tussah silk inserted into a velvet cushion.*
Made by Jean Hodges.

5 COLOUR

Colour is an important part of life. It is all around us, yet familiarity breeds contempt to such an extent that it is frequently overlooked or completely ignored. A stone which looks dull and uninteresting lying in the gutter can have quite an array of unexpected colours when cleaned and studied closely. A shell could reveal a soft, delicate array of colours or a bright, lively one. A green leaf may in fact have touches of red or cream within it. An everyday vegetable sliced through may display many subtle colour changes. Colour can appear soft and delicate, hard and intrusive, eye-catching and appealing, calm, restless or drab and unattractive. Nurserymen's catalogues listing, for example, roses and sweet peas can be a wonderful source for encouraging colour awareness, with such subtle descriptions as 'white blushed pink' or 'yellow to creamy pink'.

Colour is highly personal and it is extremely difficult not to be affected by likes and dislikes when choosing schemes. It also has physical and emotional properties. As with other forms of embroidery, moods and feelings can be expressed in smocking by the choice of colour. One person may tend towards an arrangement of soft muted tones whilst another will choose bright, jazzy colours. The use of colour can only be learnt by experiment and personal experience; it is all too easy to fall into the trap of constantly using 'safe' colours rather than taking a chance with an unfamiliar scheme.

An experiment well worth trying is to take a simple smocking design, such as a small border pattern, and carry it out in a variety of colours and thickness of threads. Suggested possibilities to try are:

- bright colours;
- subdued colours;
- dark colours;
- light colours;
- one colour contrasting with the background fabric;
- a colour exactly matching the background fabric;
- tones of one colour.

A colour worked in a thick thread on a coarse background can give an entirely different effect from the same colour worked in a fine thread on a fine background. A shiny thread will pick up the light and therefore appear brighter than the identical colour in a matt thread. It is interesting to alter the scale of the design and observe any colour differences. The choice of stitch can also have an effect on the colours. Rows of outline and cable stitch will appear more intense than open, lacier stitches such as single wave or diamond stitch.

The proportions of colour used in a design are important. By changing the sequence of tones and colours within a stitch pattern the result can be completely altered. The amount of a particular colour, and its placing in relation to other colours within a scheme, give different results. For example, work a scheme in red and green where there is more red than green and then change it to see how it looks with more green than red.

Choose the number of colours required and work them on a sample, arranging them in a different order. See which of the colours stand out clearly and also what happens when you use a dark colour. Look not only at the darkness of the stitchery but to see if the actual colour is still obvious. If you have used a dark green, can you still detect the green, or has it just become a dark blur, as can sometimes happen with smocking? The effect may be different when you use very fine threads and fabrics. Owing to the lack of bulk in the finer threads, the intensity of colour is lost and darker tones may be necessary to compensate and achieve a comparable effect.

Select the most satisfactory and the most unsatisfactory result from your samples and try to analyse why one works and the other does not. (NB. If the tones are arranged as dark, medium and light the result can be more pleasing than if they are placed dark, light and medium. A pattern with the tones of colour in sequence will usually appear more attractive and acceptable than one in which they are out of order, as the pattern can then seem restless.)

Fabrics and threads are affected by the intensity and angle at which the light catches them, and the colour will change depending on their textures. Matt, plain fabrics such as wool or linen remain fairly constant, while shiny surfaces such as satin and those with a definite pile like velvet or corduroy will change perceptibly with the light. Shiny surfaces will appear lighter or darker than they really are; pile fabrics will change according to the way in which they are used. When used vertically with the pile running up they look darker, whilst they appear lighter when used horizontally or with the pile running down. Interesting effects can be obtained by changing the direction of the pile within a piece of work. Having worked a sample, remove the gathering threads and view the work from all directions in front of a mirror (this gives the feeling of distance). Observe the shadows cast and see if the work has more impact with the tubes running vertically or horizontally.

Shot silk, with the weft of one colour and the warp of another, can be very vibrant and needs careful handling. The sheen on the surface of the silk and the difference in the colours of the weft and warp will change the tones according to the way in which the fabric is turned and smocked. One colour will dominate, according to the position of the light, and obviously this is an important factor in the choice of colour for any stitchery. This again emphasizes how necessary it is to work samples to determine the desired effect. Honeycomb stitch, triple honeycomb stitch or diamond stitch may be found to be most suitable, manipulating the fabric so that its full beauty is exploited.

The type of light falling on a colour can also play an important part. A colour viewed in bright morning light may look quite different under artificial light. It is therefore advisable to choose and match colours under the lighting conditions in which they are to be seen. Most shop assistants will allow customers to take goods to the natural light before making a purchase. Care should be taken when working smocking at night, especially where different tones of one colour are being used. It may be found useful to list and number the colours in daylight, when tonal qualities can more easily be assessed.

In view of the general linear effect of the stitches, colours used in smocking cannot always be blended in quite the same way as with other forms of embroidery. This is why the number of colours used within a piece of work should be carefully considered and related to the colouring of the background fabric. As experimentation may have shown, too many colours can have a restless, jarring effect, thus ruining the main concept of the technique. The shapes made by the tubes in the background are also an important factor. These should not be obscured by the overwhelming impact of colour. A subtle textural effect can be obtained by using a self colour such as cream thread on a cream fabric. Added impact can then be given by choosing a shiny thread for working on a matt fabric or a matt thread on a shiny one. Highly dramatic effects can be produced by using black, red or royal blue on a white fabric. A monochromatic scheme can be used with tints, tones and shades of one colour. For example, light and medium green stitchery on a dark green fabric.

Muted or greyed colours such as dusky pink are often easier to combine than the brighter colours, but whatever colours are chosen, it is the relative amounts in which they are used that is important. As already suggested, a close study of nature can suggest perfect colour schemes, especially if the proportion in which each colour appears in the flower, leaf, shell or other object is followed within the piece of work. If the predominating colour is used for the background fabric, the contrasting colours and tones will blend for the stitchery.

If a colour scheme appears dull, it may be due to equal tones being used in equal proportion so that they merge. Touches of a different tone or colour may well help to liven up the scheme. This can be achieved by adding small areas of satin stitch, bullion knots or small flowerettes. Selected areas of impact can often be more effective than taking a single colour methodically through a row.

White is frequently incorporated in a design to give added emphasis and interest. Most thread manufacturers now produce a brilliant white and an off-white within their colour range. Care should therefore be taken when deciding which white to choose to give the desired effect. This is particularly important when the fabric being smocked has an overall white background, or large areas of white within the pattern. If the fabric is creamy white, a brilliant white thread could dominate and upset the balance of the design, while an off-white thread on a brilliant white background could look dirty. Having said that, a brilliant white thread worked on a true cream fabric can be quite stunning.

In short, the clever use of colour will not only turn the commonplace into something quite exceptional but will also give excitement and drama to a piece of work which might otherwise arouse no interest. As already stated, colour is very much a matter of personal perception, and it is not always easy to select the combination which will achieve the desired effect in the finished article. It is important to stress, therefore, that a full appreciation of the possibilities of using colour can be achieved only by experiment and by being adventurous. It is in this way alone that the real contribution of colour to the enjoyment of one of our chief senses, sight, can be fully appreciated.

When designing a stitch pattern it is essential to plan the design and work a sample first. The number of tubes, as against the number of stitches, can then be carefully counted to ensure accurate placing. For example, a wave which has five stitches up and five stitches down will be worked over ten tubes for each repeat. An extra tube should then be added to each end to complete the design. If the main pattern is counted in this manner, any smaller stitch designs can be fitted into the number of tubes being used.

95 *A highly textured effect can be created by using outline, cable and surface honeycomb stitch in a simple design suitable for a collar, yoke or cuff.* (Jean Hodges)

The beauty of smocking relies on the way in which the stitches bend and group the tubes into ever-changing forms. When using a plain fabric and a matching thread the effect will become purely textural. Emphasis should then be placed on the way in which the stitches and tube patterns interact to create a variety of designs. The combination of stitches used will hold the tubes open or closed to form varying patterns. These background patterns, as well as the actual stitches, should be observed and taken into account when building up a design. The unstitched areas are as important to elasticity, tonal effects and overall patterns as the stitching itself. If all the stitch rows are crammed tightly together, the background pattern will be obscured

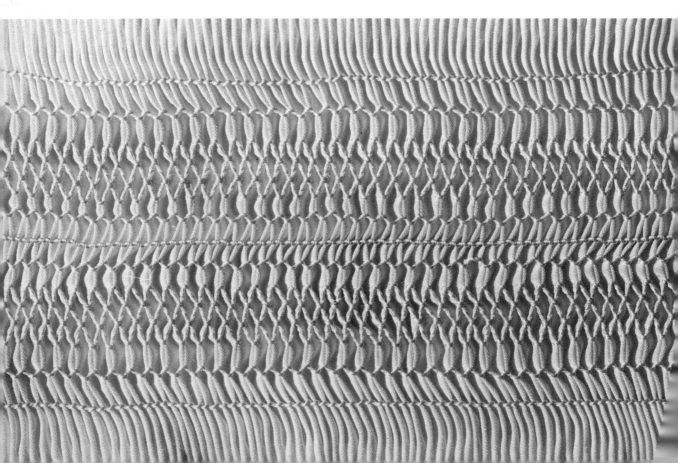

96 *Sketchbook ideas using simple stitching.*
(Ros Chilcot)

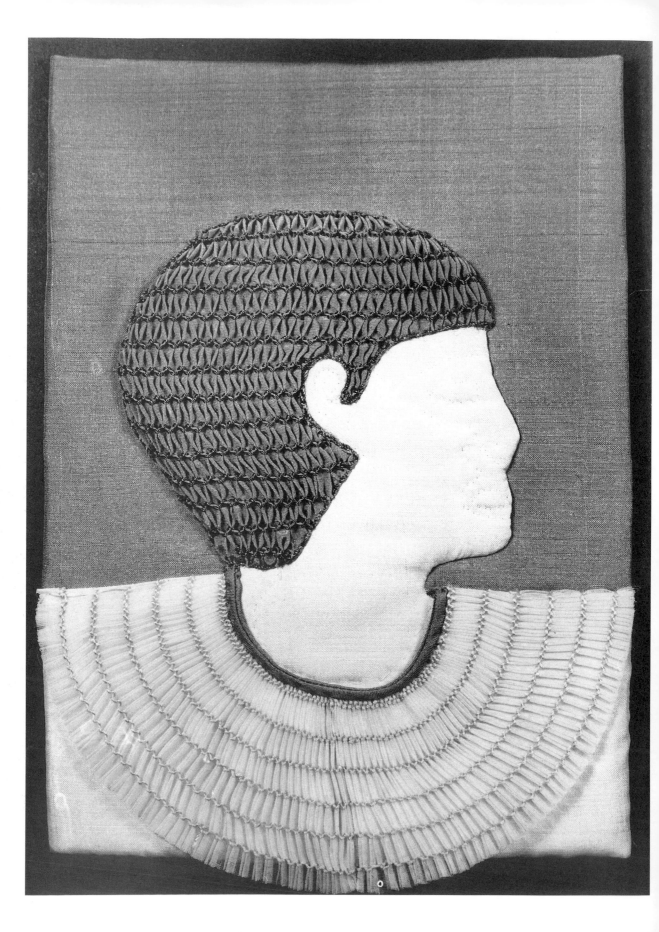

and with it the intrinsic beauty and elasticity of this embroidery technique. Likewise, too many different stitches can cause a fussy, restless effect, so avoid the enthusiastic inclusion of every known stitch in one piece of work – unless it is to be used as a sampler! It is better to use three, or possibly four, basic stitches and rely on the way in which they are combined to achieve an interesting design.

Experimentation with the various stitches will soon reveal how background designs can be built up. Spaced at intervals and in varying proportions, decorative bands and patterns are easily created. Work a row of cable stitch followed by a second row of cable on the next gathering thread, placing the up stitches of the second row opposite the down stitches of the first row. Work a third row of cable stitch over the third gathering thread, but this time have the up stitch corresponding to an up stitch of the row above.

The tubes between the first and second rows will group together to form strong straight lines, whereas the tubes between the second and third rows form a 'V' or chevron pattern. The profile of an Egyptian head shown in fig. 97 illustrates this particularly well. The design relies entirely on the way in which the cable stitch moves the tubes, giving a strong contrast between the hair and the collar. These effects are further emphasized by the light catching the tubes and by the fact that the eye is not confused by the use of different colours.

A deep panel of spaced cable stitch, frequently found on traditional smocks, can give the appearance of knitting (fig. 98).

When rows of wave stitch are worked, leaving a space between each row, the tubes move to the side to create fan shapes.

BALANCING A DESIGN

The complete pattern should be well balanced; it should not be too large or widely spaced on a small garment, nor so small that it is completely overlooked on a larger article.

Where a symmetrical design is planned, it is important to have the largest motif centred in the

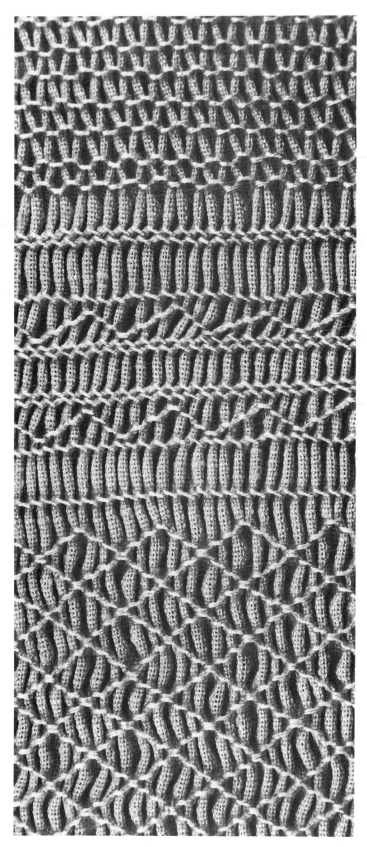

97 *'Egyptian Head.' Quilting combined with cable stitch smocking.* (Gillian Jenkins)

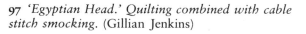

98 *Panel from a modern smock front.*

middle of a row or area. To ensure that the pattern will finish at the same point in the repeat on either side of the panel, count to the centre tube and mark with a coloured thread. Find the centre of the actual design, and starting at this point, smock from the central tube towards the right-hand side. Turn the work upside down and smock from the centre towards the other side, retaining the continuity of pattern. To avoid having joins at this central point, take a length of thread sufficient for the whole row but only pull enough through at the first stitch to complete one half, leaving the other end hanging. You may find it easier to wrap this loose end round a pin to keep it out of the way. After turning the work, thread the needle with the loose end and continue working. Once the sequence is established, the smocking can be started in the usual way from the beginning of each row.

POINTS

Smocking can easily and effectively be shaped into points. Cable, vandyke, honeycomb or surface honeycomb stitch, used either as part of an overall design, or worked as a finish to a panel, can look very attractive (see fig. 56). The pointed shapes can be worked over fabric drawn up in the usual manner with gathering threads running from end to end of each row. If transfer dots are being used, the transfers should be cut into an actual point, thus avoiding the risk of any dots showing through the unsmocked areas. The number of dots required for a point needs to be calculated so that each row has one dot less at each end, with the last row consisting of three dots to make two tubes (fig. 99).

99 *Shaping dots for a point.*

Pointed smocking can be used in many ways to add interest to a variety of garments or articles. It could extend from the cuff up a sleeve, radiate down from a neckline, or be worked in varying sizes extending from the waist to give an interesting hipline. Lampshades, pelmets, curtains and cushions can all have pointed designs incorporated.

BUILDING UP A DESIGN

Drawing and devising a smocking design is basically a simple task, yet it can be very exciting watching the different shapes and patterns gradually build up.

One line placed parallel to another will form a stripe. Lines varying in direction and joining each other will make zigzag patterns and battlementing. Units formed in this way can then be used as border patterns, repeated in rows or made into alternating arrangements. The same units can be arranged to form all-over designs suitable for deep panels, or be separated by bands of stitching such as honeycomb, surface honeycomb or diamond stitch.

Lines can cross each other to form grids or lattice patterns. Fig. 100 shows an interesting triangular pattern created by honeycomb smocking on a fabric which had previously been spray painted through a grid to give squared lines of uncoloured fabric.

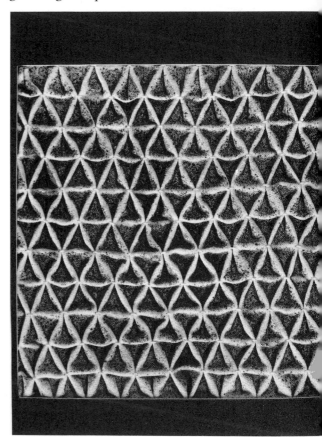

100 *For this sample, masking tape was laid on calico in a grid pattern. The exposed areas were then sprayed with fabric paint and the tape removed. By using honeycomb stitch smocking, an interesting triangle design has been formed.* (Mary Fortune)

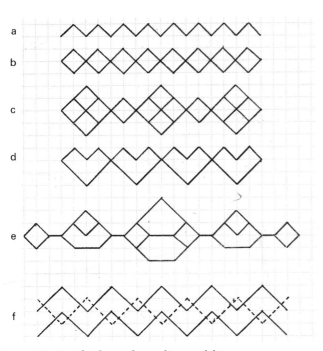

101 *Design built up from diagonal lines.*

Triangles can be placed side by side to form zigzag (chevron) patterns, or placed together to form diamonds.

In order to start designing stitch patterns, try drawing a row of chevron shapes on to graph or squared paper, as in fig. 101a. Draw a second row underneath to form a series of diamonds (fig. 101b). This gives the beginning of a pattern. Diamond stitch could be used to interpret fig. 101a, giving a small zigzag shape. Wave stitch would give a deeper effect. Fig. 101b could be interpreted in many ways – a double row of diamond stitch, two rows of wave stitch to form a trellis, closely stacked cable to form a diamond-shaped block, honeycomb or surface honeycomb stitch worked within a diamond shape. These are a few examples worth considering for this design, although experimentation could produce more. If, when working these patterns, the results do not quite come up to expectations, do not reject the sample completely; it may well suggest other ways in which an idea or shape could be developed at a later date.

A heart shape can be formed using two diamond stitches and a wave underneath. Such motifs can be used in isolation or strung together to form an interesting border. The same basic shape can also be interpreted by combining small and deep waves, giving a larger unsmocked area which could then be

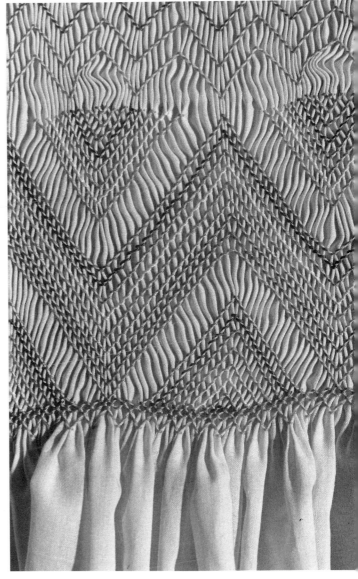

102 *Rows and blocks of wave stitch used in a simple design. The areas of close wave stitch give greater emphasis to the patterns formed by the unsmocked tubes.* (Jean Hodges)

further embellished with the occasional flowerette or bullion knot rose. Such a shape can be particularly effective when used at the bottom of a design, with two or three rows of close, deep waves, graduated in colour, giving impact and balance to a scheme.

As already noted on page 37, the scale to which the design is worked can also have a significant effect. For example, as in fig. 102, the small-scale waves at the top of the sample give a completely

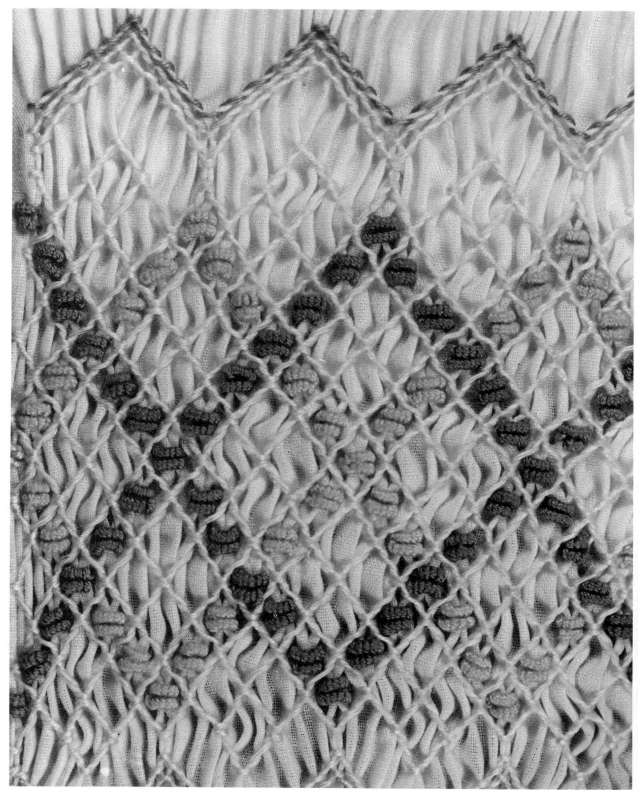

103 *Bullion knots are used to create a*
secondary pattern on a background of diamond
stitch. (Jean Hodges)

different impression from the larger waves which form the main pattern.

Another way of using diamond shapes is as shown in fig. 98, where the stitching is worked in one colour, leaving the spaces free. The spaces could then be worked in the same stitch using a different colour. Alternatively, the space could be decorated with a small motif such as a flowerette or bullion stitch rose, or with satin stitch or beads. Colouring in or shading some of the areas on the design drawings is a further possible alternative which could help to suggest a wealth of ideas.

BACKGROUND DESIGNS

Any zigzag stitch worked in rows will give a trellis effect. This can form an interesting design on its own or, according to the type and size of stitch chosen, can form a background for further embellishment and pattern design. A panel worked entirely in diamond stitch can have a secondary pattern of diagonals, diamonds or random areas brought out by the use of bullion knots, satin stitch or bullion knot roses (fig. 103). This secondary design can be worked in one colour, in tones, or in a contrasting colour. The effect of ribbons being threaded through the background can easily be achieved in this manner.

SHAPE

Where there are lines, by definition there must be spaces in between. Where lines join up the spaces are enclosed and thereby shapes are formed. It is important to be able to recognize these shapes, especially in smocking, which is essentially dealing with lines and the effects they can have on each other, as well as on their background.

It may be easier to consider shapes if they are thought of in terms of positive and negative. Having shaded in areas of a design, consider these as the positive, to be filled with stitching. The unshaded areas are then the negative or background areas, and are left unstitched. Using the same shapes, reverse the positive and negative and a totally different effect will emerge.

Charts 16 and 17 show the same design handled in these contrasting ways, and it will be seen how totally different they look, although exactly the same number of tubes and stitches are involved in each case. Looking at fig. 104, notice how the stitched area (positive) causes the unstitched tubes

104 *The background shapes formed by the blocks of cable stitch become the important part of this border design. A triangular pattern of bullion knots worked into the diamond stitch area adds interest.*
(Jean Hodges)

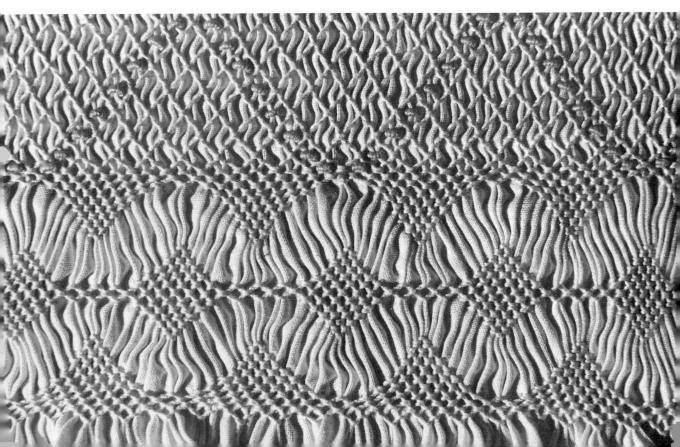

105 *Greek key pattern.*

106 *Dress worked in two tones of peach with a light and dark green Danish flower thread on peach polyester/cotton fabric. Herringbone stitch and small ribbon bows complete the design.* (Jean Hodges)

(negative) to stand out in a very strong manner, to such an extent that they become almost the most dominant part of the design.

A simplified version of the Greek key pattern could make an interesting border or be formed into a square for a cushion, wall hanging or box top. The

two designs in fig. 105 show the effect of reversing the positive and negative patterns. The shaded area could be worked in surface honeycomb stitch, with reverse smocking (see page 113) being used for the unshaded parts. Alternatively, the whole design could be worked using two colours or a light and dark tone of one colour.

The panel of the child's dress shown in fig. 106 is built up using half the border design for the top of the pattern, with a row of zigzag cable to soften the line. The zigzag cable also enables the colouring to merge into the central area of diamond stitch. The border at the bottom (chart 25) gives weight to the design as well as firmly controlling the gathers at the waistline. By filling the triangular and diamond (positive) areas with stitchery, the colour of the fabric can be obscured, throwing the unsmocked (negative) area into relief and causing it to become more prominent than it would be if the design had been worked purely in a wave stitch.

For this particular garment it was found necessary to add a small surface herringbone stitch above the smocked panel and around the collar and sleeves, in order to balance both the design and the colour scheme.

REPEATING LINES OF SIMPLE STITCHES

The use of multiple rows of a simple basic stitch is one of the easiest ways of filling a space, yet at the same time it can produce quite dramatic effects.

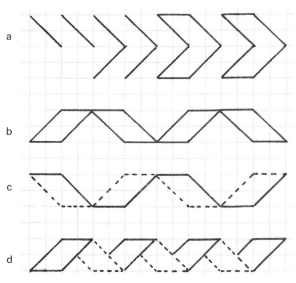

107 *Building up simple designs with the possible use of two colours. The shapes can be formed by the use of cable and wave stitch, or the area within the shapes may be filled with stitchery.*

Excellent examples can be found on traditional smocks, where a single or very limited number of different basic stitches were used in block designs.

In a more creative form, rectangular blocks of surface honeycomb stitch worked in contrasting colours could be used to suggest the effect of a basket weave, as shown in fig. 108. The tubes in the

108 *Basketweave design.*

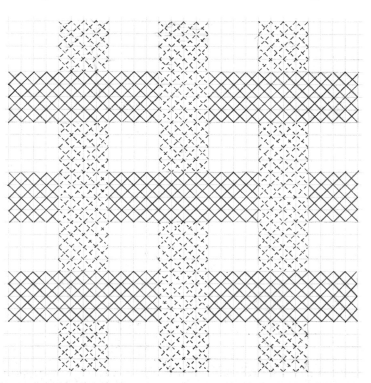

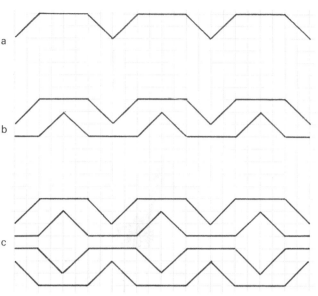

blank areas are held in place by rows of cable stitch on the back.

A considerable variety of other ideas are possible using repeating lines in block patterns, and are well worth further development (see fig. 109).

109 *Building up designs with wave and cable stitch.*

110 *'Easter Egg'. A straight strip of smocking has been joined and moulded over a polystyrene ball. The ends are drawn together and neatened with a decorative ribbon bow.* (Heather King)

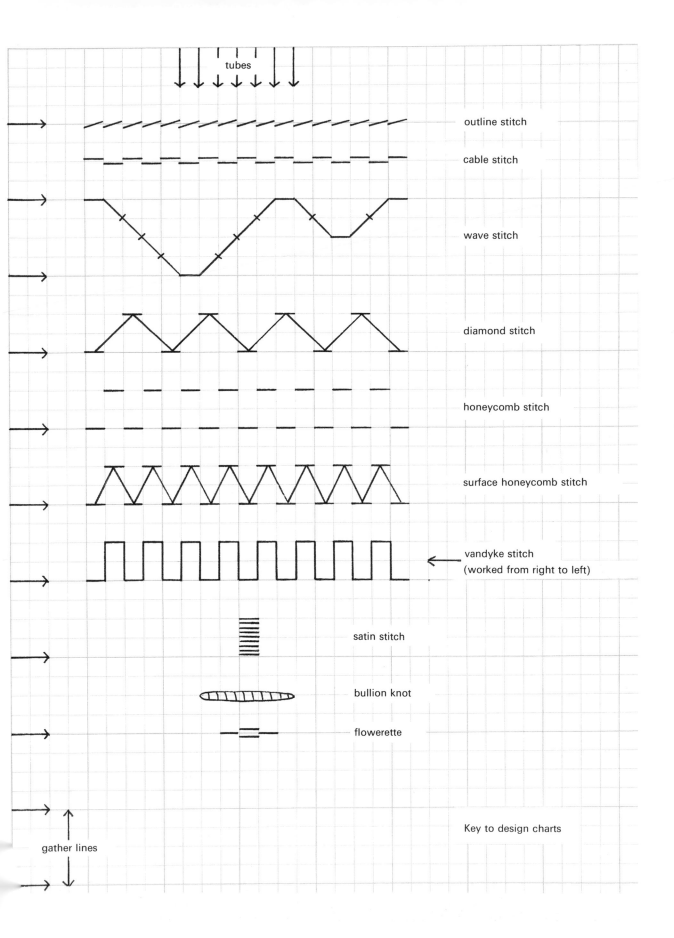

tubes

outline stitch

cable stitch

wave stitch

diamond stitch

honeycomb stitch

surface honeycomb stitch

vandyke stitch
(worked from right to left)

satin stitch

bullion knot

flowerette

Key to design charts

gather lines

Design charts

On the following pages will be found a number of charted smocking designs which, it is hoped, may encourage further inspiration and development. Some suggestions are made as to their possible use, although many more will emerge as each design is adapted or worked in a different colour or type of thread.

The designs are shown on squared paper. Each vertical line represents a tube, with the short line indicating where a stitch goes through a tube. The heavy horizontal lines indicated by arrows represent the gathering threads.

The smocking stitches are indicated on the charts as shown in the key on page 79. All are worked from left to right except vandyke and feather stitch, which are worked from right to left.

Border designs can be used on their own where only a shallow design is required, such as the front of a child's dress, as a narrow insert, or combined to build up into deeper panels.

111 *Sampler showing interpretations of a simple border design in cable and diamond stitch. The top border is worked in a matching thread. The second example is in a dark and medium tone mauve cotton perlé No. 8. The third is of the same colouring, but in a coton à broder which, being a finer thread, gives a lighter appearance. The bottom design is worked in a pink and a mauve silk buttonhole twist, this time alternating the colours.* (Jean Hodges)

Chart 1 *A simple design which can have a bead or french knot added for extra sparkle.*

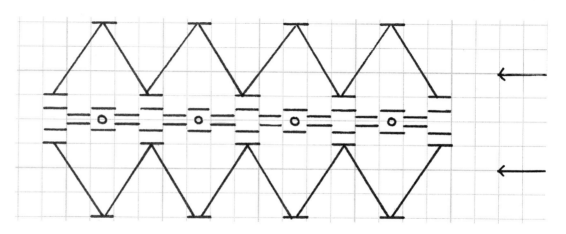

Chart 2 *This design can be worked in a number of ways, as suggested in fig. 111. Satin stitch can be added for extra impact if required.*

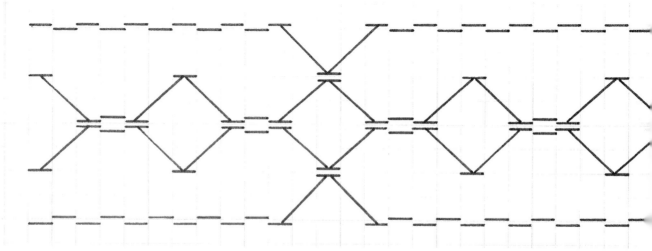

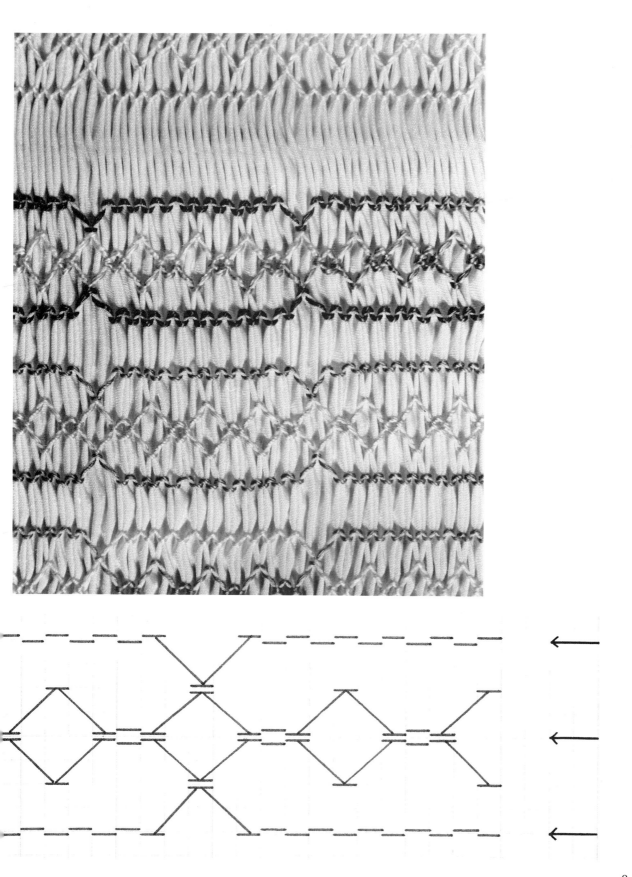

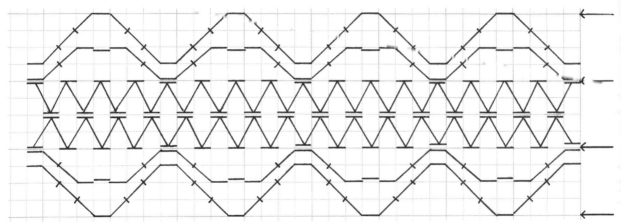

Chart 3 *A very effective design when worked with the thread matching the background colour to give a lace effect (fig. 112).*

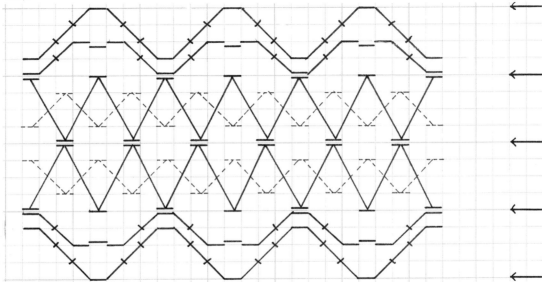

Chart 4 *The smaller diamond stitch can be worked in a different colour or type of thread.*

Chart 5 *Interesting patterns can be built up by varying the size of the diamond stitch. The broken line indicates where a different colour or thread could be used effectively.*

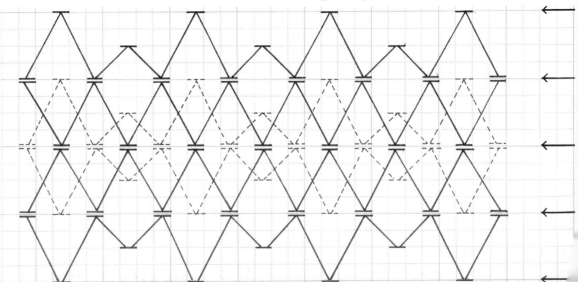

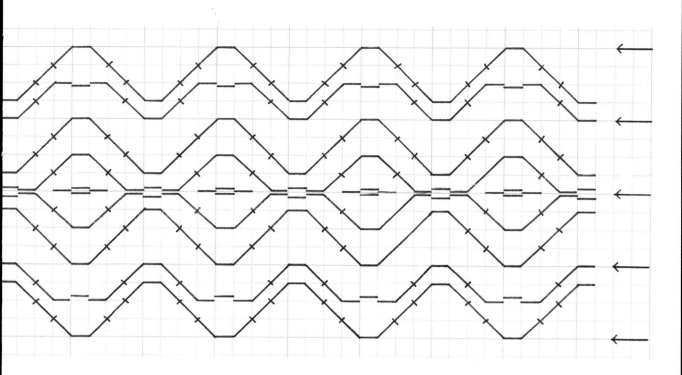

←
←
←
←
←

Chart 6 *(See also figure 112.) The design can be repeated to build up into a deep panel. It could also be used on a cuff or the front of a child's dress.*

112 *A feeling of lace laid over tubes can be created by working border designs in a matching thread. The white panel inserted into this turquoise evening bag shows three separate designs worked in white coton à broder with touches of dark turquoise as a highlight.* (Jean Hodges)

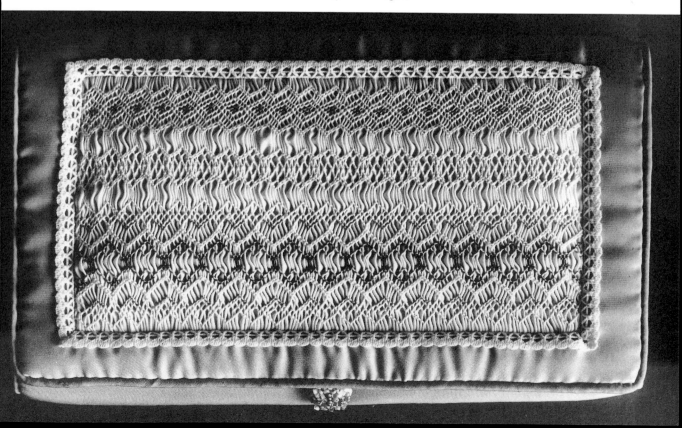

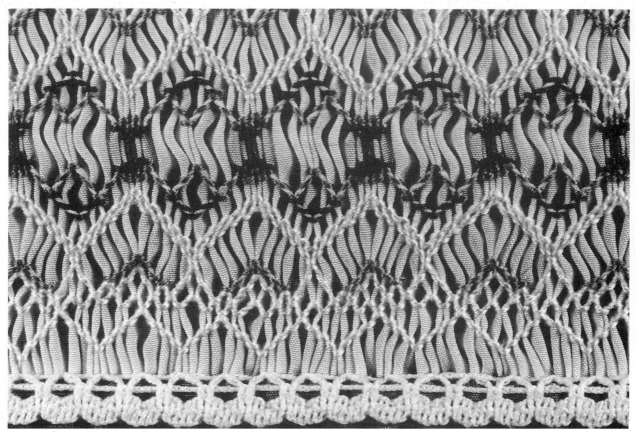

113 *Detail of fig. 112. The way in which the tubes move and form their own patterns gives added interest to the design.*

Chart 7 *Small flowerettes, bullion knots or satin stitch can be used in the centres.*

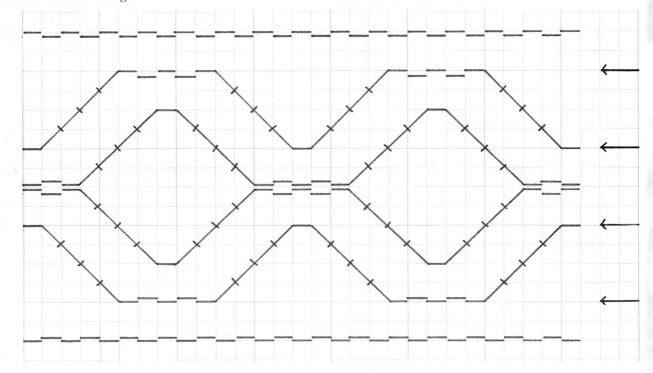

114 *Separate borders are built into an all-over design for the front of a dress.* (Jean Hodges)

115 *Border design. The cable and wave stitch outline is worked first and then the area is filled in with surface honeycomb stitch, wave stitch and small flowerettes.* (Jean Hodges)

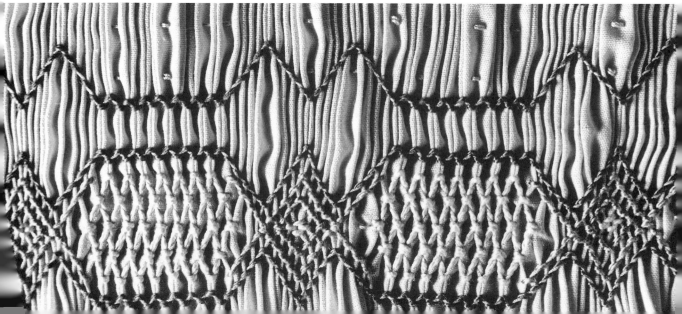

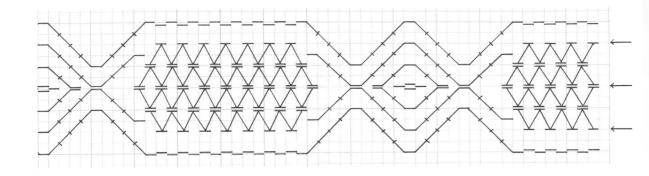

Chart 8 *Design taken from an American Indian headband (fig. 114). Each of the surface honeycomb blocks could be worked in a different tone to give a subtle colour change when used over a wide area such as a belt.*

Chart 9 *The dotted lines indicate where a different colour is to be used. The surface honeycomb stitch makes this a very elastic design (fig. 47).*

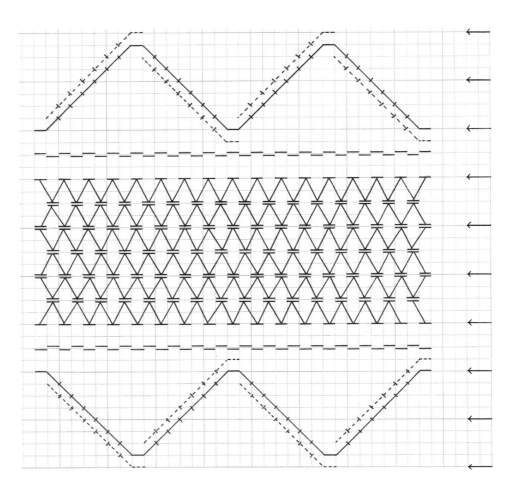

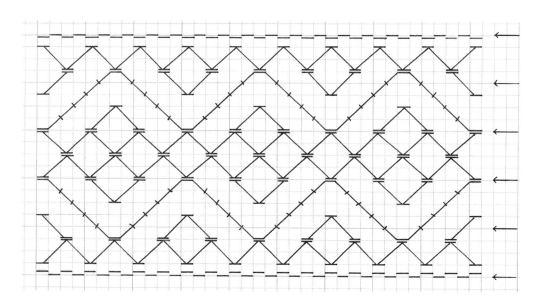

Chart 10 *The border design will easily repeat by omitting the cable stitch rows to form a deep panel and works well as an insertion. Beads can be added in selected areas.*

Chart 11 *A design which is effective when used with the tubes running horizontally (fig. 82).*

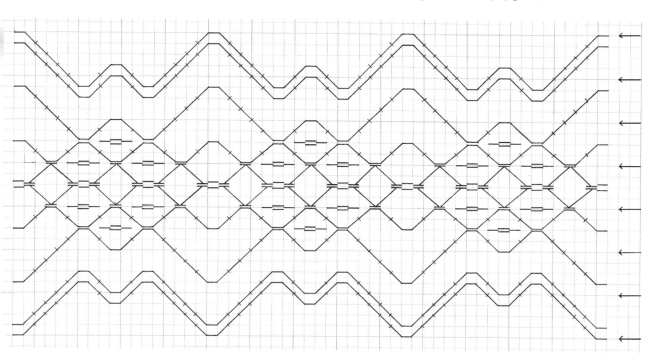

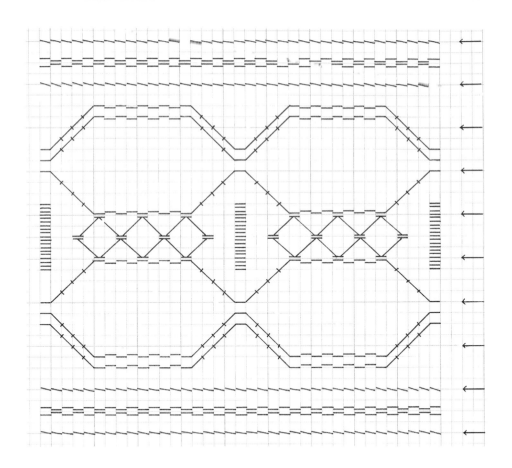

Chart 12 *Design charted from the 1930s smocking shown in fig. 5.*

Chart 13 *A versatile design which can be used on its own or built up as indicated by the dotted line.*

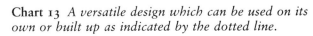

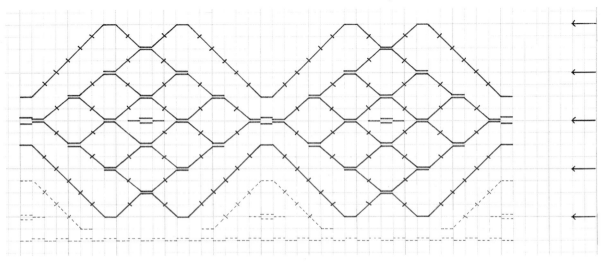

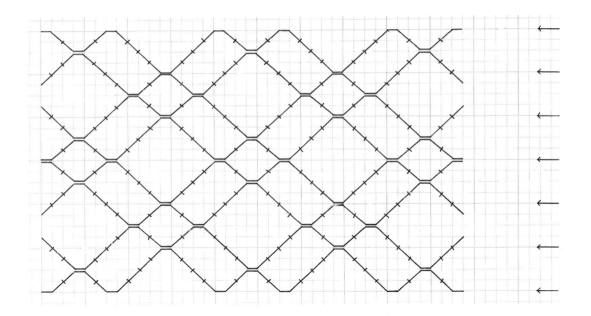

Blocks of smocking can be used for borders or will build up to cover larger areas suitable for bags, boxes, cushions, garments, panels and wall hangings. When working in blocks, the fabric should be turned in order to smock backwards and forwards to fill in the shape.

Chart 14 *An effective but simple background design, as used in fig. 87. The whole panel can be worked in one colour, or a slight tonal change can be made on each row.*

Chart 15 *The areas between the two chevron shapes can be held on the back with cable stitch (see page 152) or filled with diamond stitch using a contrasting colour.*

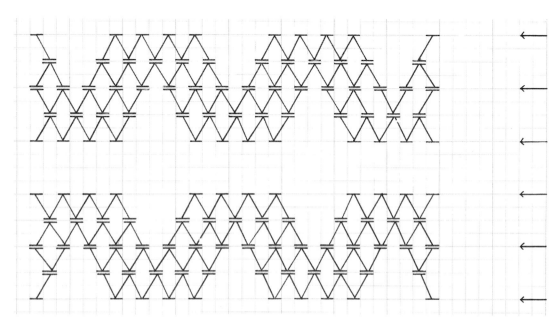

Charts 16 & 17 *The same design is used alternating the positive and negative (see page 75). The unsmocked areas should be held on the back with cable or diamond stitch.*

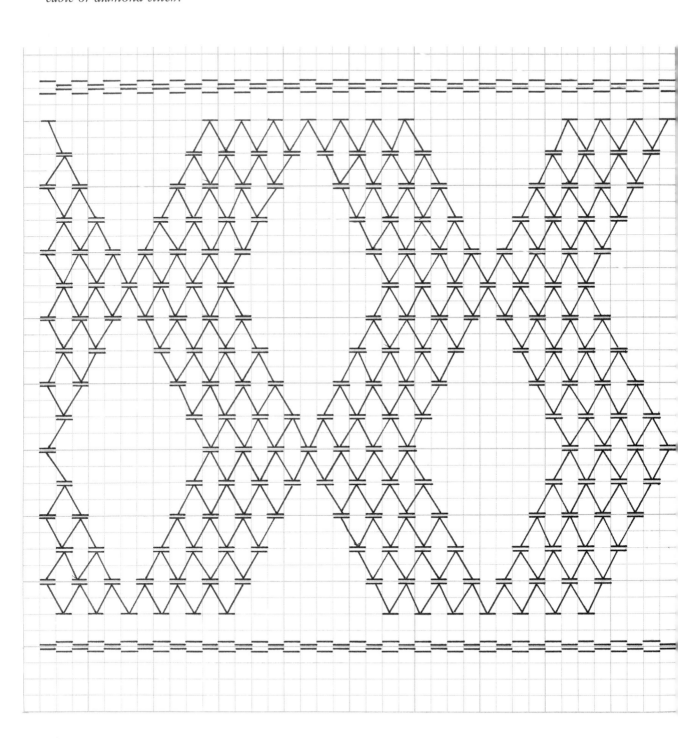

90

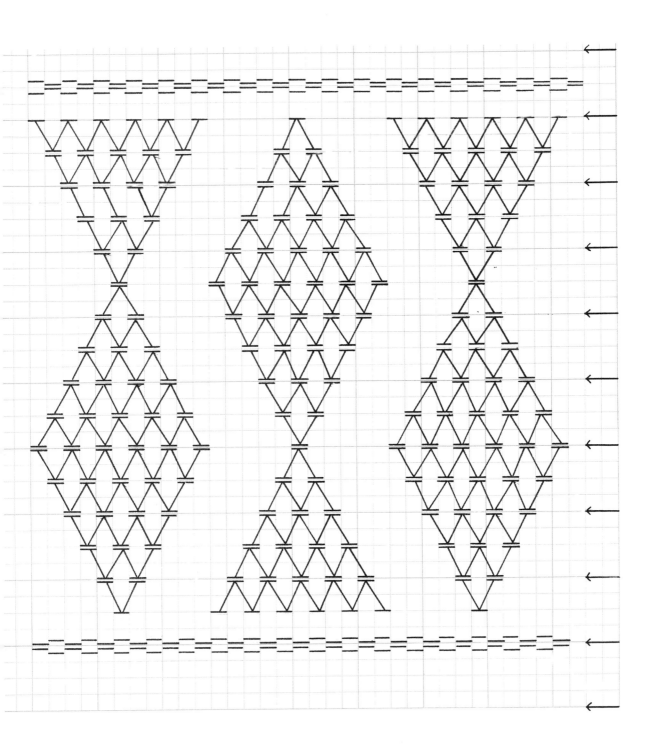

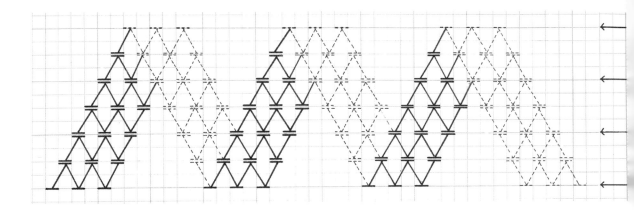

Chart 18 *A three-dimensional effect is obtained by using two colours or tones, as indicated by the broken line.*

Chart 19 *The inner lines can be worked in a different tone to give added depth. Surface embroidery stitches could be added within the large hexagonal areas.*

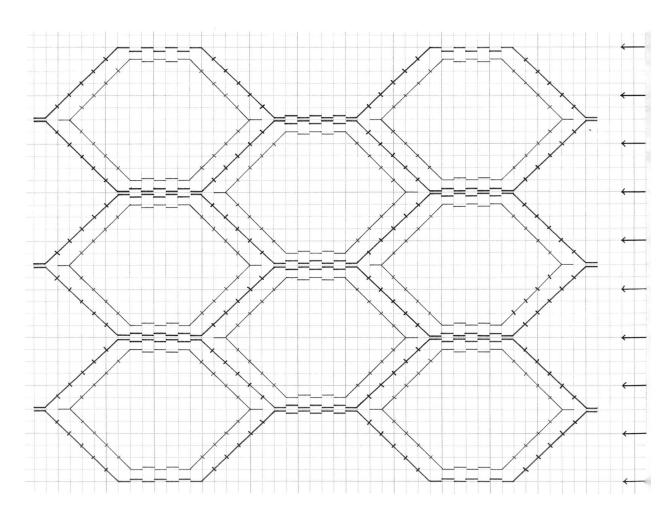

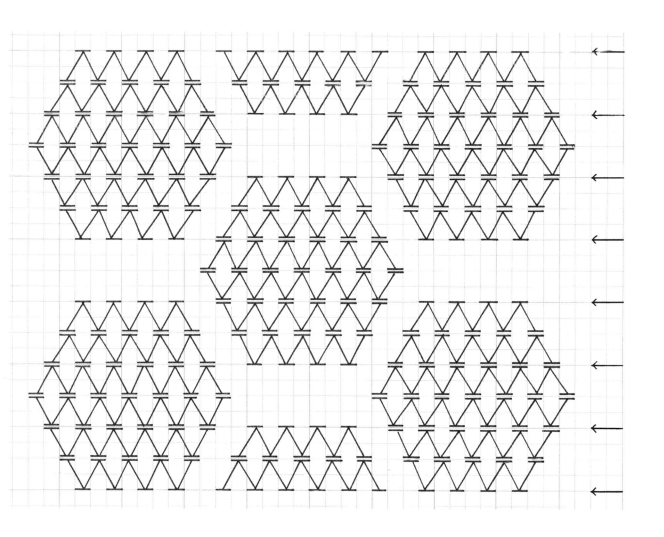

Chart 20 *This design is particularly suited for working on heavier fabric such as satin with 1.5 cm ($\frac{1}{2}$ in.) deep tubes.*

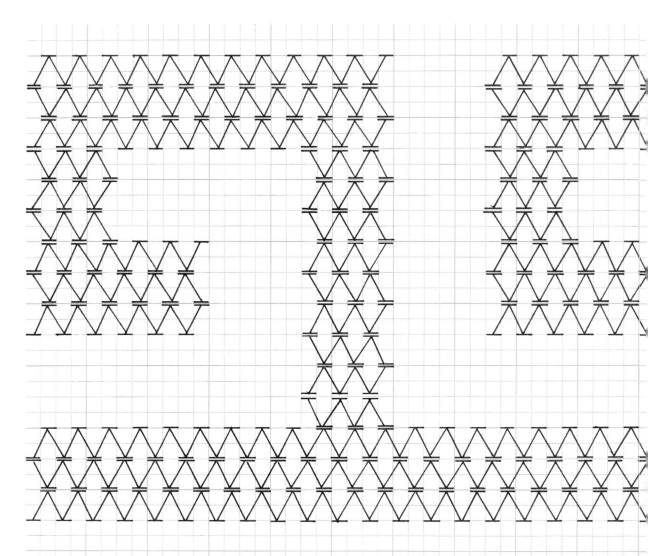

Chart 21 *A Greek key pattern adapted as a border. Work the surface honeycomb stitch first, turning the fabric for each row. The unsmocked areas are then held with stitches on the back.*

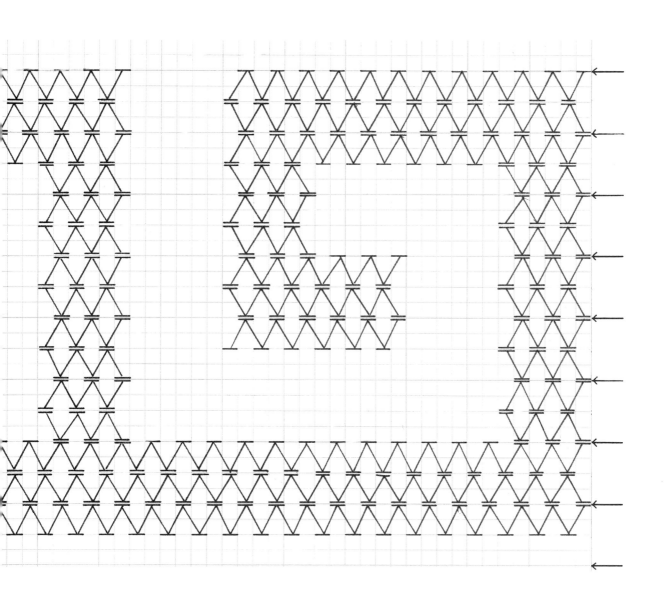

116 *Smocked herb cushions.* (Jean Hodges)

Chart 22 *The central area can be condensed or extended to fit the depth of smocking required.*

Deep panels can be used on clothing, cushions, bags and wall hangings. The designs can be worked to any scale.

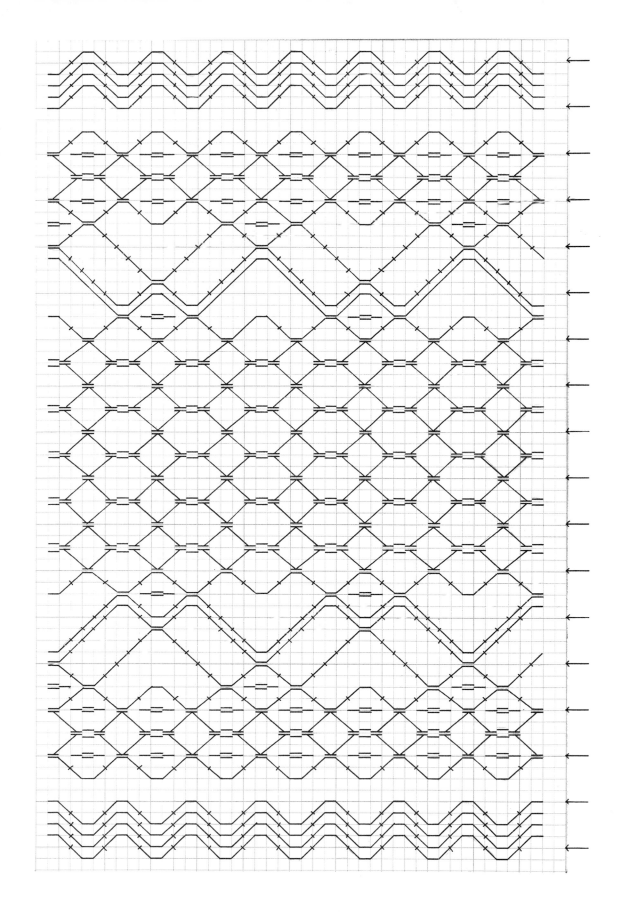

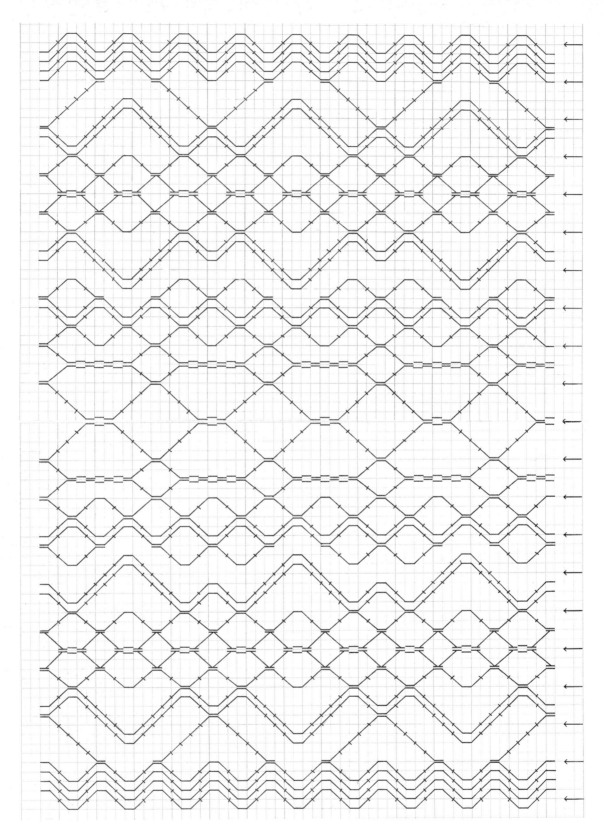

Chart 23 *The design illustrated in fig. 117 is built up from border designs. Small flowerettes or bullion knots can be added as required.*

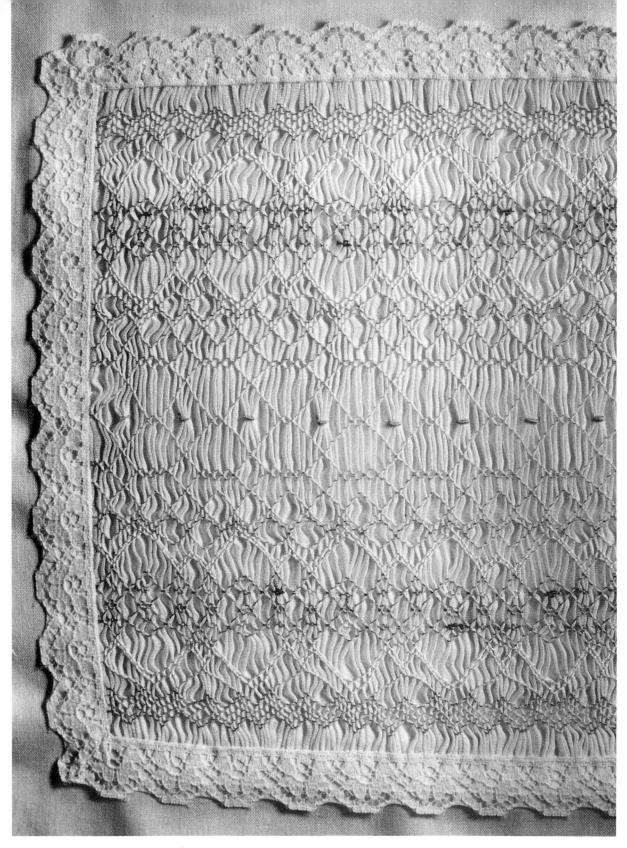

117 *Detail of a cushion from fig. 116. The smocking is worked in sewing-weight silk thread on fine cotton voile.* (Jean Hodges)

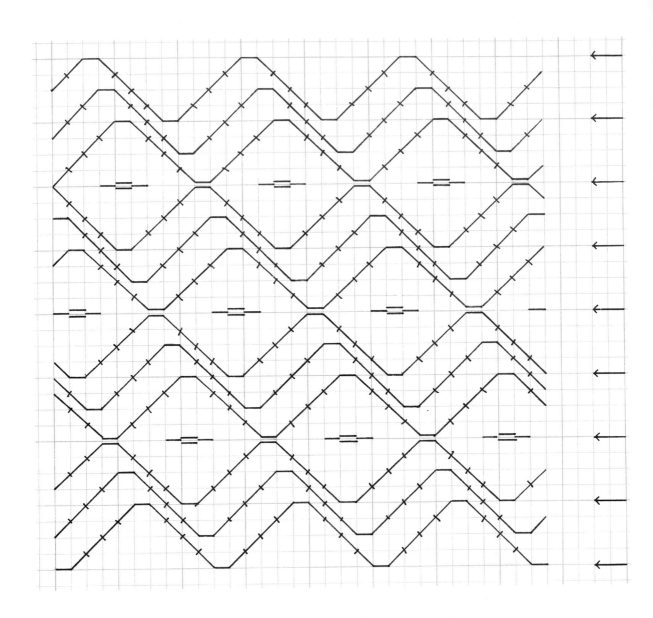

Geometric shapes can make very interesting designs.

Chart 24 Staggered wave stitch can form an interesting all-over design, especially when used with the tubes running horizontally. The feeling of movement could be further enhanced by introducing different tones or by varying the type of thread used for each group of waves.

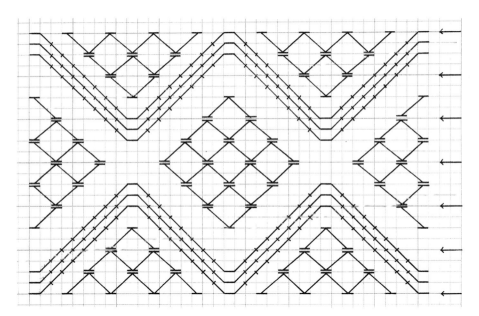

Chart 25 *This can easily be turned into a deep panel. The deep waves are a dominant part of the design and can be effective when worked in three tones (fig. 106).*

Chart 26 *This design, based on diamond and cable stitch, is particularly suited for use where colours are to be blended. The original idea shown in fig. 58 was worked in tones of blue, but would be even more appropriate where contrasting colours are being used. The optical mixing of the colours when they are worked over each other gives a more gradual and subtle introduction to the next colour and avoids the feeling of cutting a design into bands.*

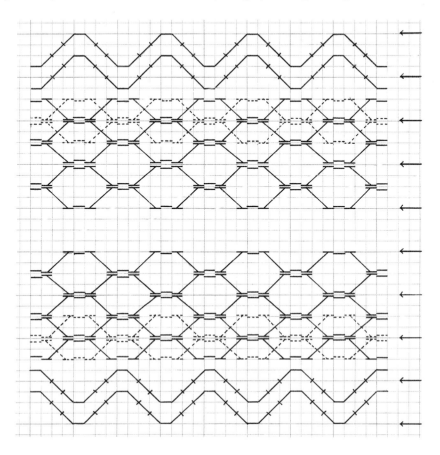

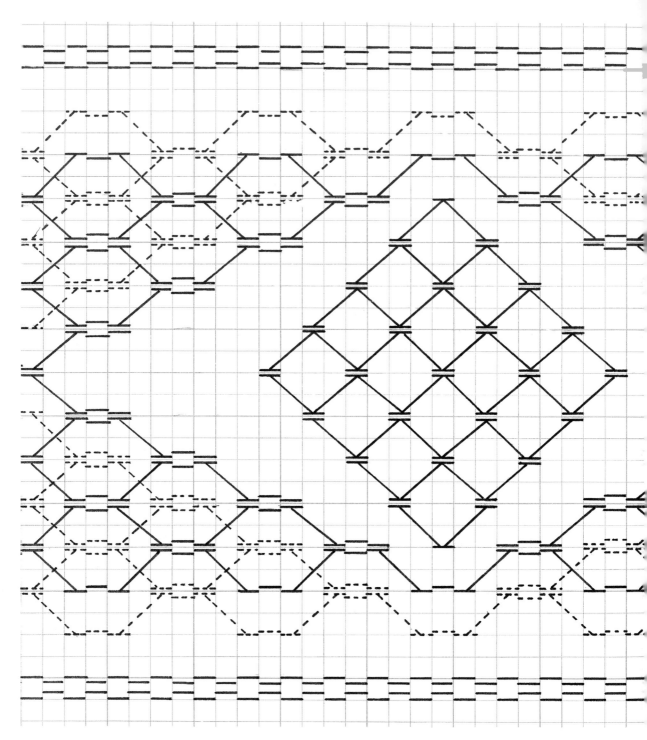

Chart 27 *Used as an insert, illustrated in fig. 16, it could also be used as a border. It is a firm design.*

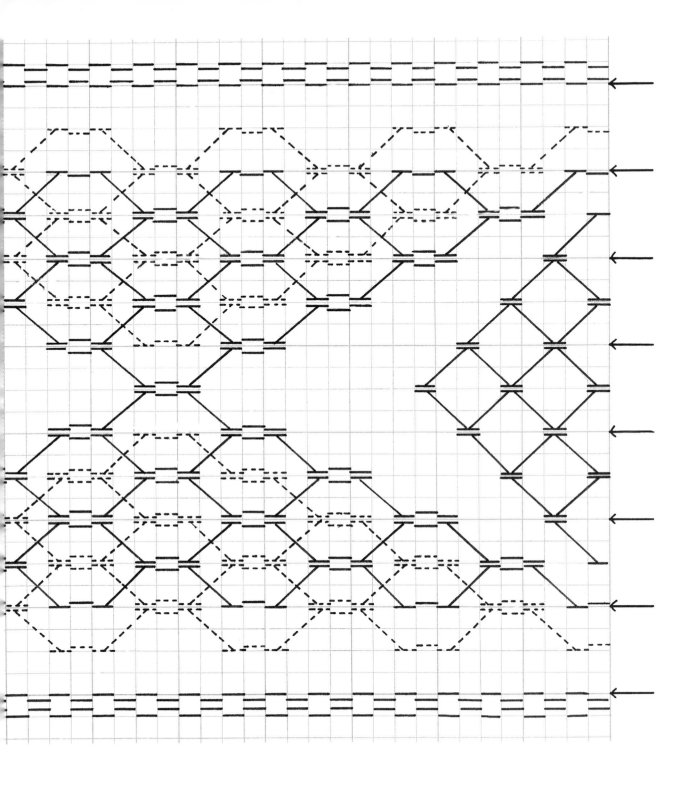

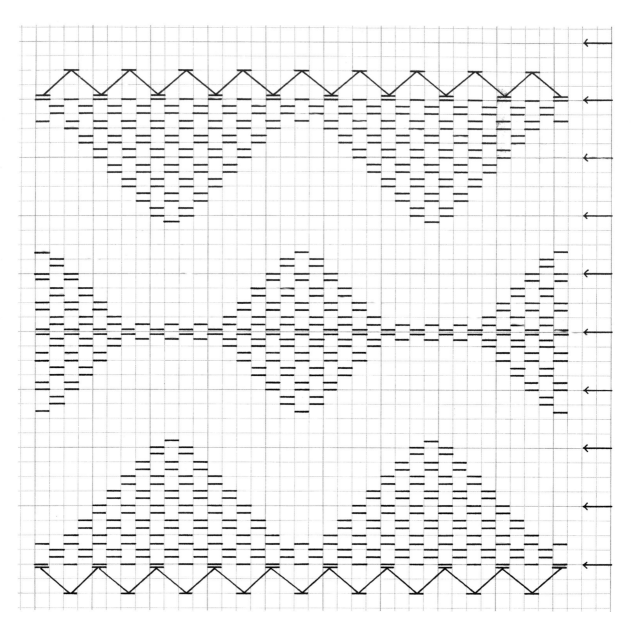

Chart 28 *The unsmocked area has the appearance of circles and stands out against the cable stitch blocks (see fig. 104).*

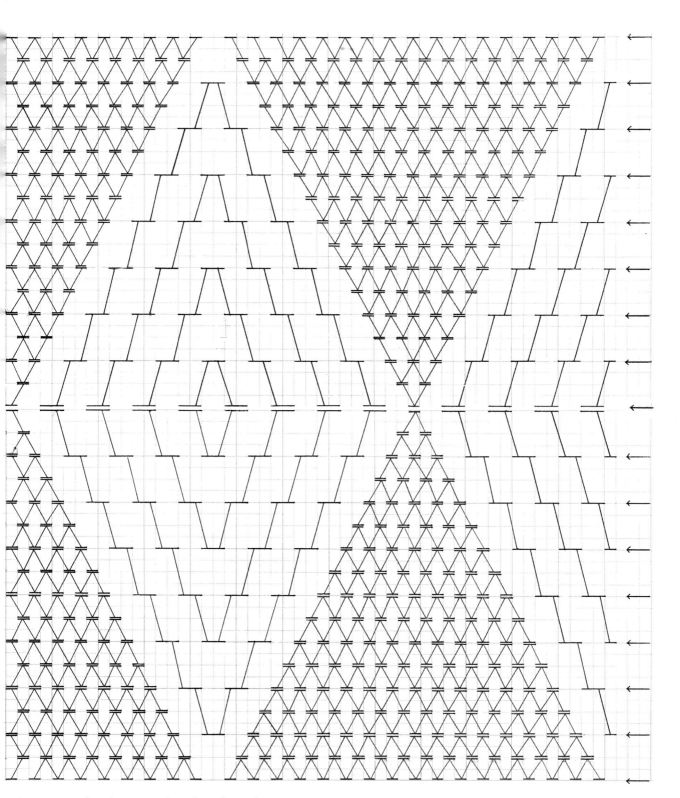

Chart 29 *Surface honeycomb and triple surface honeycomb combine well in a design. The diamond shape should be worked as described on page 114.*

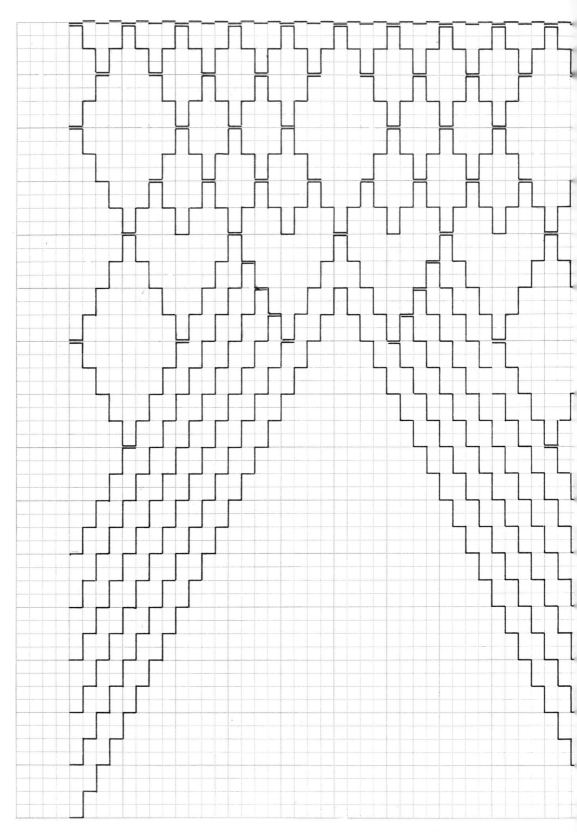

Chart 30 *Diagonally worked vandyke stitch, illustrated in fig. 56. Suitable for a neckline, skirt or wherever the tubes are required to fan out whilst being held firmly.*

Pointed designs can be used to finish a panel of smocking, to fan round a neckline or similar curve, or to radiate up a sleeve or wherever else it is desirable for the tubes to splay out.

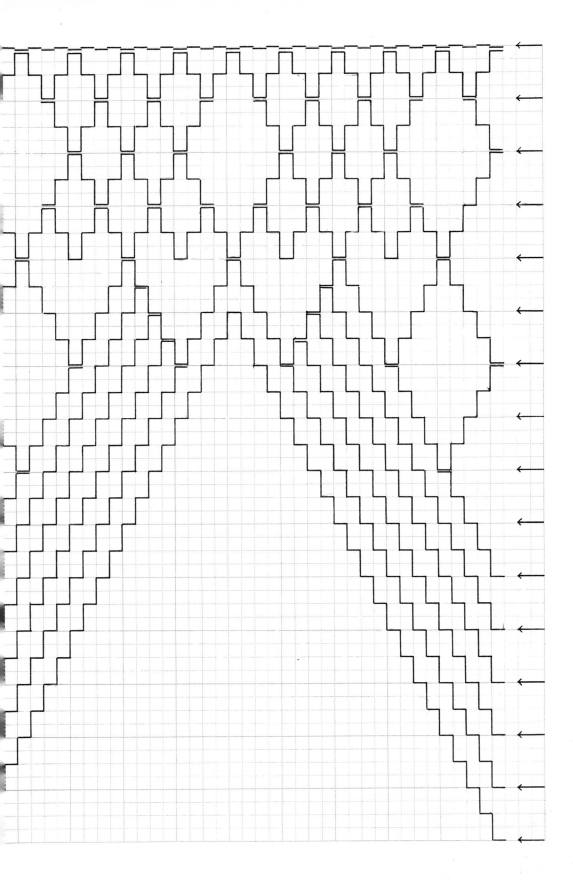

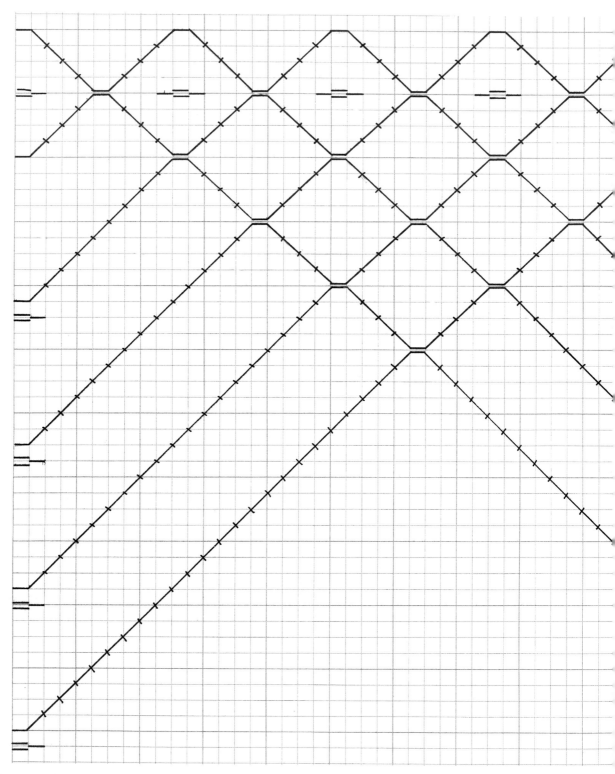

Chart 31 *The wave stitch design is illustrated in fig. 25. This is effective when stretched round a curve, as petal shapes are formed. It can easily be adapted to a different size and would be very attractive used for baby clothes or a circular cushion.*

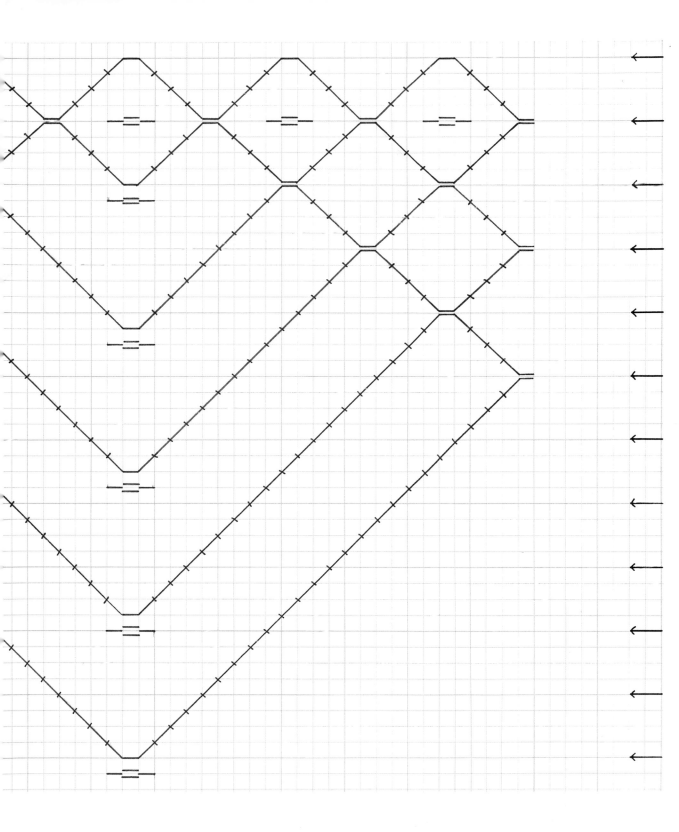

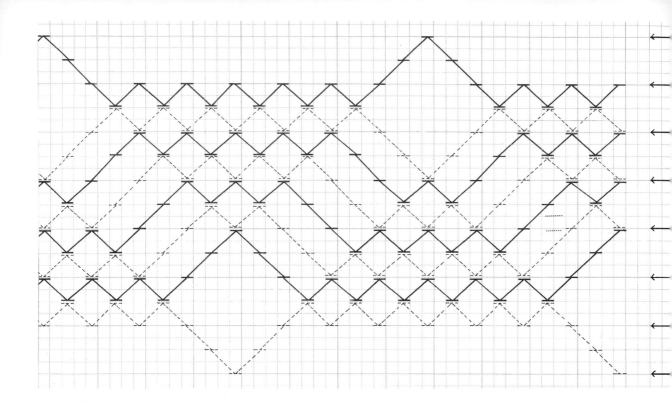

Chart 32 *Diamond and wave stitch. The broken lines indicate how each row is worked.*

Chart 33 *The vandyke border could be effective where a firmer pointed finish to a deep panel of smocking is required.*

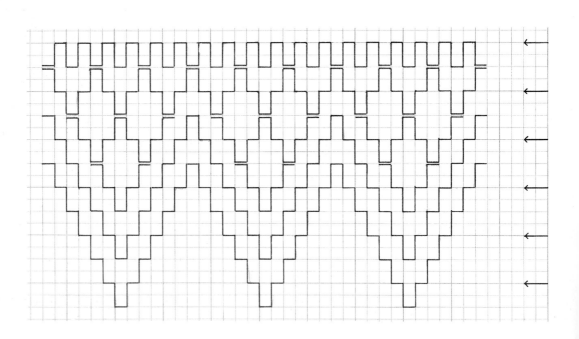

7 FREE SMOCKING

Until recently, smocking was seldom incorporated into embroidered hangings and panels, although most other traditional methods of embroidery have been adapted to keep pace with contemporary ideas and designs. For far too long, this beautiful technique has been confined to the fashion world and clothes for young children in particular. Its textural qualities and adaptability make smocking an exciting and valuable addition to free expression of movement and feeling within embroidery. The rhythmic and rippling appearance of the folds as they catch the light, together with the shadows they cast, can create stunning effects and should be exploited to the fullest possible extent.

It is easy in the constant search for something

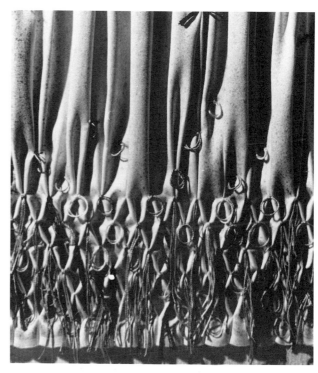

118 *Detail from 'Four Seasons' panel.* (Mary Fortune)

119 *'Four Seasons.' Honeycomb stitch with added ribbons and threads worked on spray-painted silk.* (Mary Fortune)

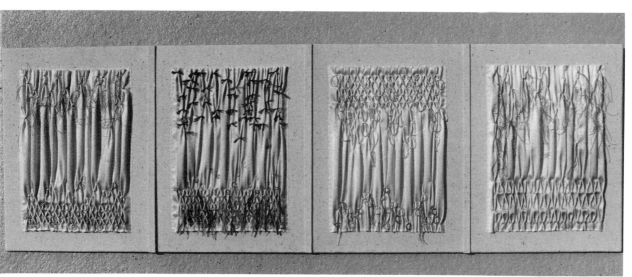

120 *Random-spaced reverse smocking gives the feeling of tree bark.* (Anne Wilson)

'new' in embroidery to lose sight completely of the purpose and construction of a technique in such a way as to make its origins entirely unrecognizable. It is to be hoped, however, that this will not be the fate of modern smocking.

As has already been discovered, smocking is a highly textural and decorative form of embroidery. The stitches and ideas so far encountered in this book have emphasized the need to work with the tubes accurately gathered on the straight of grain in order to retain the perfection of the technique. However, once the technique is fully understood, it is possible to extend and develop smocking by 'bending' (but not destroying) these rules in such a way that new interpretations and greater emphasis on the textural quality can be exploited whilst still maintaining the intrinsic beauty.

REVERSE SMOCKING

Take a piece of smocked fabric, turn it over and look at the back. Notice how, when it is stretched very slightly, the tubes will bend and ripple, forming ever-changing patterns. This is the basis of reverse smocking.

Reverse smocking can open up new ideas and ways of interpreting designs. The tubes are held by smocking stitches on the back, leaving the front for further development. This method is also employed

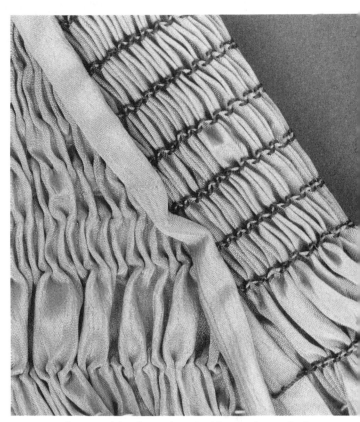

122 *Sample turned back to show cable stitch worked on the reverse.*

to hold tubes where there are large unsmocked areas on a design which could otherwise distort or flatten (see page 34). The technique has the same basic gathering preparation as traditional smocking, except that the fabric is picked up above the dots instead of on them (fig. 121). After the gathering threads have been secured, the tubes are held in place by working rows of smocking on the wrong side, using an appropriate weight and colour of thread. The stitching is worked along the actual line of dots, avoiding the gathering threads, as they could become entangled in the stitching. Avoid picking up too much fabric when working on the back, as the stitches may be inclined to show on the front and so interfere with and spoil the finished effect. Cable stitch will produce firmly controlled gathers, while honeycomb stitch will give greater elasticity. Wave stitch of varying size creates a feeling of movement, and can form an interesting and sympathetic background for use with motifs, geometric shapes or pictorial designs worked on the front. Experimentation with the holding stitches will produce a wide variety of interesting effects on the right side.

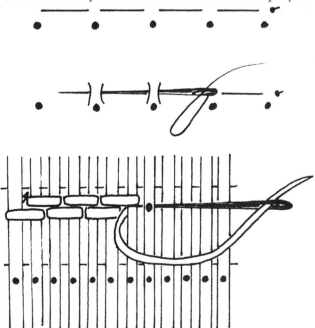

121 *Picking up dots for reverse smocking.*

Very interesting and unusual textures can be obtained by combining areas of surface and reverse smocking within a single panel. It will be noticed that the surface smocking recedes whilst the reverse smocking actually comes forward. This feature can be incorporated into fashion in a most exciting way and will also give textural interest to a cushion, quilt, box top, panel or wall hanging. The main bodice of a dress worked in a simple all-over stitch such as diamond, diamond and cable combined, or trellis, with an area left on the front to be reverse smocked, can give the feeling of an inset yoke or panel. The spun silk dress shown in fig. 125 is an example of this idea, with rosebuds added to enhance the design. A softer fabric such as polyester/cotton will exaggerate this effect in a garment even more than the spun silk.

A cushion or a quilt could have a diamond shape worked in honeycomb or triple-honeycomb stitch in the centre, surrounded by reverse honeycomb or reverse triple-honeycomb stitch. This combination would give the effect of the diamond being set down within the surround. If the diamond was worked in a reverse stitch with the surround worked on the surface, the centre would then stand forward. A central panel worked in this manner using a satin or similar weight fabric surrounded by quilting would make a luxurious bed cover.

When a diamond shape is worked, the centres will need to be marked to aid the positioning of the smocking. If the smocking stitch requires two tubes to be taken together, as in diamond or honeycomb stitch, then the centre channel should be marked. If, however, triple honeycomb stitch is being used and three tubes are to be taken together, then mark the top of the centre tube. The central gathering thread also needs to be marked. It may be found easier to start at the centre top and gradually work down towards the central gathering thread, turning the work to save constantly stopping and starting.

COMBINING TECHNIQUES

Smocking has a richness and texture which may be missing from some other forms of embroidery. These qualities allow it to combine with certain other techniques, often as a complete contrast, so that each will complement and enhance the other.

Quilting is just such a technique. The sharply etched and tactile appearance of smocking is the perfect foil for the subtle, rounded contours of

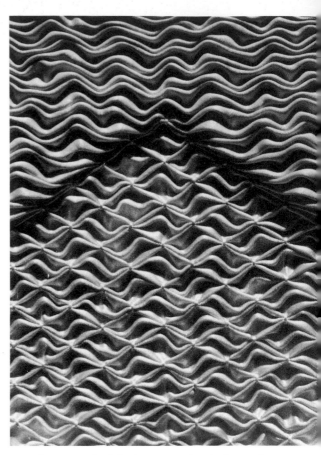

123 *An area of triple honeycomb stitch recedes against the surround of triple honeycomb stitch worked on the reverse.*

quilting. An added bonus is that both forms of embroidery are ideally suited to a wide range of garments and articles.

Italian quilting can be used not only in conjunction with smocking, but also as a means of forming the tubes over which the smocking is worked. Fig. 127 shows organza layered over silk with channels machined and filled with coloured wool, which were then randomly smocked. This method would be ideally suited to the designs shown on page 121.

Tucks of all sizes can be delightful when incorporated into almost any article. They are extremely versatile and will blend perfectly with smocking, as the stitched tucks can take the place of gathered tubes. There is also the great advantage that only selected areas need to be stitched, and therefore bulk is kept to a minimum. Honeycomb stitch would appear to be the most appropriate stitch to use so as not to mar the beauty of the tucks,

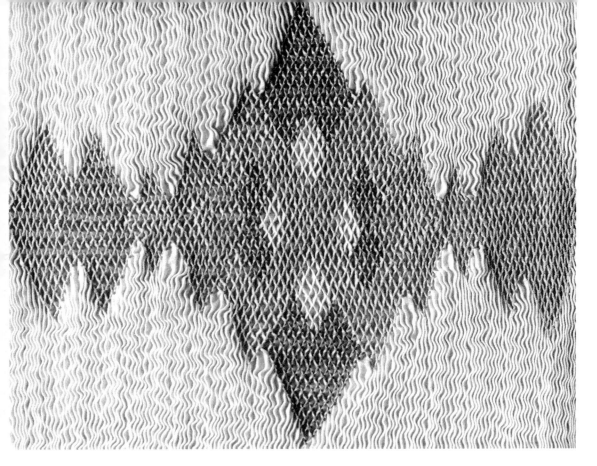

124 *Blocks of surface honeycomb stitch worked against a background of wave stitch on the reverse.* (Jean Hodges)

125 *Spun silk dress. The bib effect is created by reverse smocking.* (Rose Glennie)

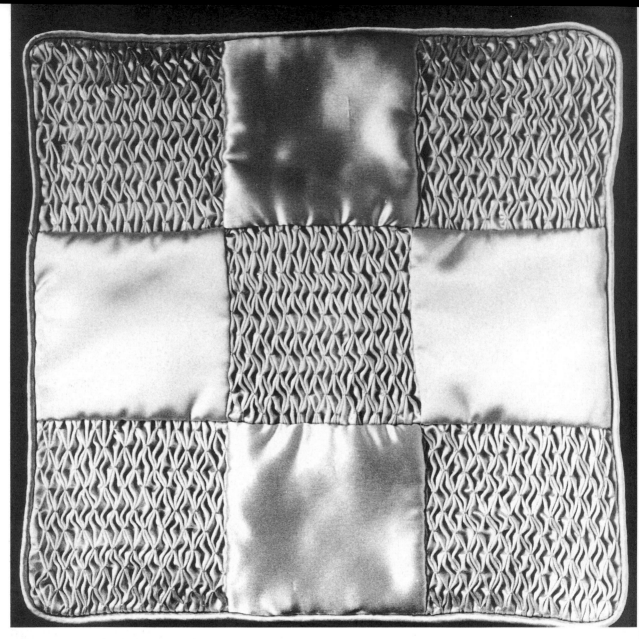

126 *The richness of triple honeycomb stitch on cream
satin, combined with the smoothness of quilting,
could be incorporated into cushions, quilts, garments
or wall hangings.*

although it is worth considering other stitches if you
are seeking a particular effect.

When using fine or transparent fabrics, the
narrow tucks can have coloured wools, ribbons or
cords threaded through in areas to complement the
smocking. This idea would look particularly
attractive on a fine blouse, dress, christening robe
or baby pillow.

The panel in fig. 128 shows the use of larger-scale

127 *Shadow Italian quilting combined with
smocking. The fineness of the top fabric allows the
colour of the quilting thread to show through and
give extra interest to the random honeycomb
smocking.* (Mary Fortune)

128 *Machine stitched tucks on calico with fabric
paint applied in alternate stripes before smocking.
The cells are filled with straight stitches, french
knots, eyelet stitch and beads worked over
transparent fabric to create the background scene.*
(Anne Wilson)

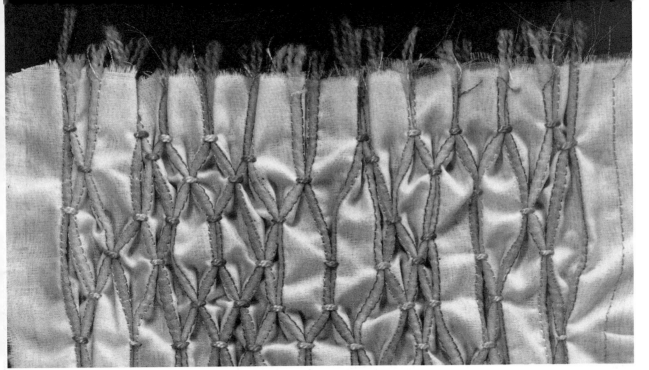

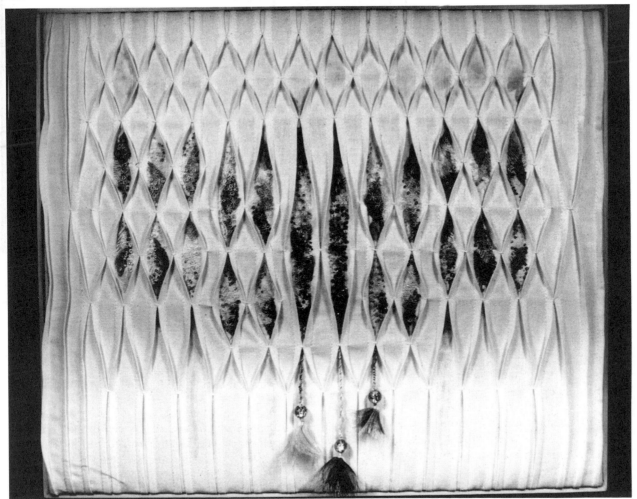

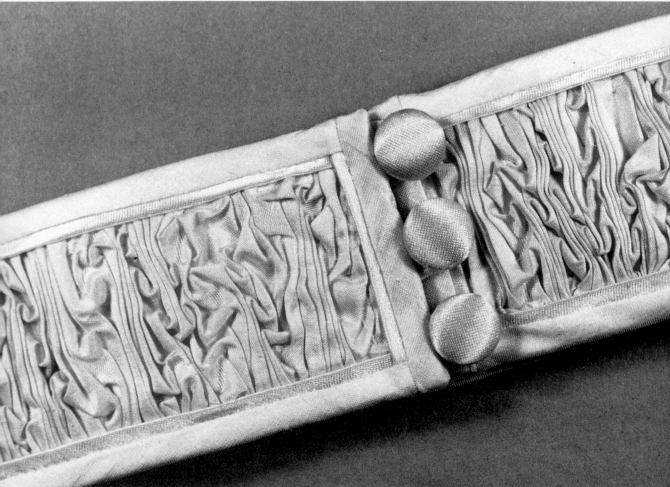

129 Silk belt. Randomly gathered silk gives the appearance of wood grain, and bias-cut binding with a straight trimming inset complements the highly textured effect. (Ann Andrew)

130 Detail of fig. 129.

tucks in a highly successful manner. Calico was machine stitched to form even tucks, then fabric paint was applied in alternate stripes. Selected cells formed by the smocking were filled with straight stitches, french knots, eyelet stitch and beads worked over transparent fabrics. Bead and transparent fabric tassels complete the design.

DESIGN SOURCES

Many things which are all around us in everyday life can spark off ideas for smocking designs. Buildings and architecture; the natural landscape; trees, flowers and plants; animals; rivers; waterfalls and seascapes together offer a profusion of readily

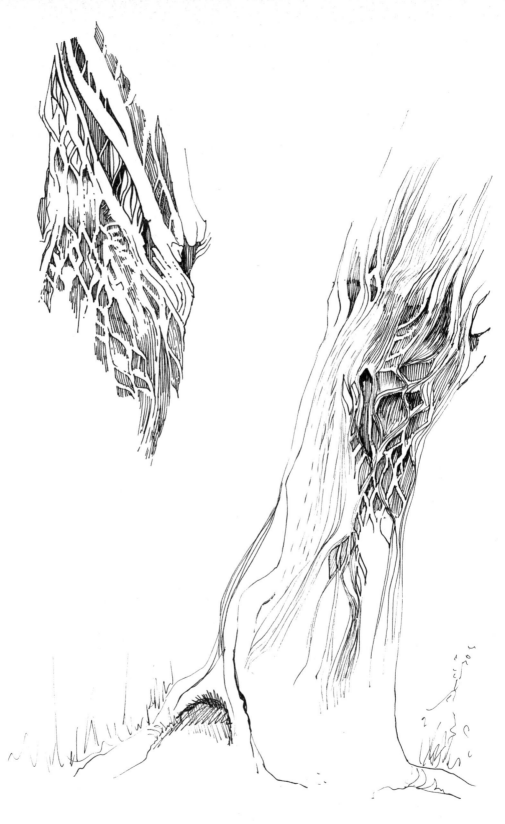

131 *Sketch of tree trunks with 'smocked' effect.*
(Ros Chilcot)

accessible subjects which can be interpreted in smocking. A sketchbook or camera kept at the ready can help in recording these ideas. Later, the drawing or photograph can provide the basis for preparing a design.

An example from the world of architecture is the three-dimensional panel shown in fig. 133, which was inspired by the decorated chimneys at Hampton Court. Surface stitchery, smocking, Italian quilting and twin-needle machine stitchery were all used to simulate the patterned brickwork so characteristic of the Palace.

The interiors of cathedrals and churches or secular structures such as classical ruins, public halls, country houses or farm buildings are equally suitable as design sources. They have a wide variety of interesting design features such as their vaulted ceilings, columns and archways, as well as the more mundane detail of their often elaborately decorated windows and doors. The sketches in fig. 134 can be used as a starting point. The stone tracery of the Gothic arch can be formed by reverse smocking or smocking over tucks. As an alternative, the ogive arch window can be created by the use of smocked Italian quilting. Firm fabric such as calico or raw silk would give the strong rounded contours to the mouldings. A non-woven interfacing can be added to the back of the fabric before gathering or tucking if this is thought necessary, to provide extra bulk. The impression of stained glass in the windows can

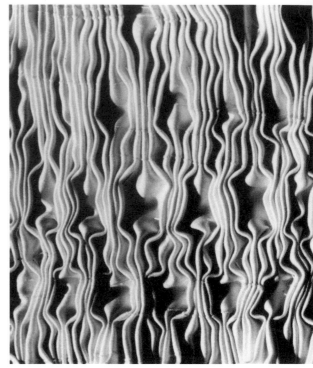

132 *Gathering threads are used in such a way as to distort the tubes and create a textured design. No further stitching is necessary, as the threads are left in place. This method is not elastic.* (Jean Hodges)

133 *'Chimneys.' Smocking, Italian quilting, surface stitchery and twin-needle machine stitching combine within the panel.* (Dorothy Phillips)

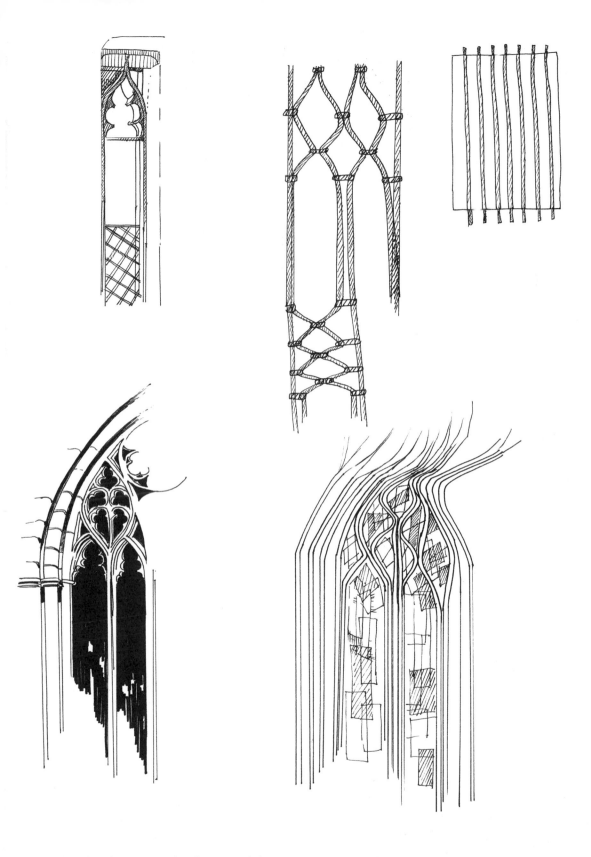

134 (a) *Sketches from a notebook.* (Ros Chilcot)

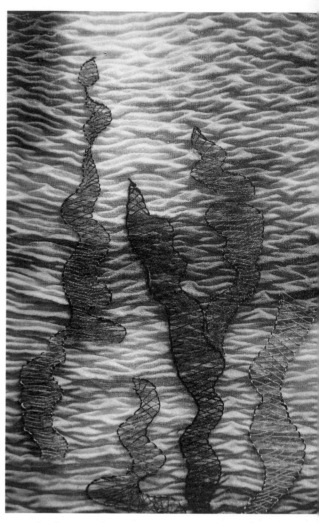

134 (b) *Sketch of Petworth House gates.*
(Ros Chilcot)

135 *Shadow work on transparent fabric laid over a reverse smocked background suggests the tranquility of gently rippling water.* (Adrie Philips)

be given by filling the spaces between the smocking with pieces of coloured transparent fabric.

The seashore, with its ever-changing patterns, provides a host of possibilities for ideas: the tranquillity of the shore at low tide with rippled banks of sand and the light glistening on the distant water; the etched surfaces of the rocks and the myriad plants, fish and crustaceans marooned in the crevices and pools.

This contrasts with the full force of the waves, whipped up by a strong wind, crashing against the rocks.

'Storm Force Ten', illustrated in fig. 137, is a good example of the feeling and expression one can achieve by the use of simple smocking stitches. Here, the powerful force of the waves is depicted by manipulating outline-stitched silk which has been dyed with a pink and a grey-blue colour. Strips of gathered organza have been added to suggest foam, with extra stitchery and beads to provide the necessary sparkle and movement. Straight stitching worked on the background fabric gives the impression of heavy rain.

136 '*River Views*'. *The gathering threads are left in the random-dyed silk to create the water. Wrapped threads form the roots.* (Joan Matthews)

Jersey fabric will smock extremely well. Owing to the weight of the material it can be very easily manipulated into ripples and swirls, making it ideal for interpreting the sand on the seashore depicted in the sketch in fig. 140.

Try gathering up a piece of jersey fabric and bending it in all directions until the desired effect is achieved. Remove any gathering threads not required, and loosen or tighten others as necessary. Gathering threads can be left in this type of work provided they are being used as part of the structure. The tubes can then be secured by smocking stitches on the back.

137 *'Storm Force Ten.' Random-dyed silk, smocked
using rows of outline stitch with extra surface
stitching and beads.* (Gillian Jenkins)

138 'White Cliffs.' Surface and reverse smocking have
been included in this panel. (Mary Morton)

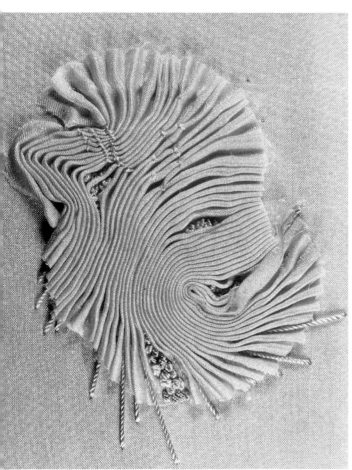

140 *Sketchbook ideas from a shoreline.* (Ros Chilcot)

139 *Fabric can easily be manipulated into ripples and swirls with the tubes held by smocking or surface embroidery where necessary.* (Mary Fortune)

141 *Plastic can be gathered to give a watery effect.* (Madeleine Millington)

142 *Surface and reverse smocking worked over patterned organza, with areas of surface stitchery and scrunchy french knots, create this watery insert in a canvas work box.* (Mary Morton)

143 *Sketchbook designs from waterfalls.* (Ros Chilcot)

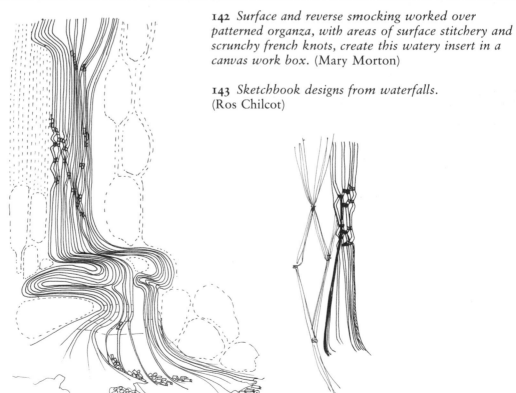

144 *Sketches of watercress beds. These could be interpreted by smocked transparent fabric over pieces of appliquéd patterned fabric, with leaf shapes applied where they break the surface. The cross patterns could be indicated by leaving in shiny or silver gathering threads across the fabric.*
(Ros Chilcot)

The smocked piece is placed on a suitable backing fabric and held in place by means of surface stitchery. Bullion knots, french knots and beads can be added for grains of sand or rock pools. Cretan stitch, herringbone stitch or elongated chain stitch can simulate the look of seaweed at the water's edge. Make sure that the direction of the stitches is in keeping with the general look and design.

The sea can then be made from lighter, more transparent fabrics such as silk and shot organza, leaving frayed edges to suggest surf or bubbles, with small beads and french knots made from Lurex thread to lend sparkle.

Many fabrics such as silk jersey, shot silk organza, georgette, chiffon and soft polyesters will drape and mould in such a way that they can best be described as 'fluid'. It is for this fluid quality that they could prove the ideal medium for interpreting the waterfall sketch in fig. 143. The feeling of weight, unrestrained natural force and sheer magnificence is evident as water drops and cascades

down a waterfall. This can be indicated in the design by holding the gathers in place with smocking on the back and catching the occasional tubes together on the front with bugle beads sewn in the direction of the water. The gathering threads can then be removed from the bottom edge, enabling the fabric to be spread out, and extra beads, french knots or suitable surface stitchery added to suggest bubbles and spray. Different colours and types of fabric can be layered together or placed side by side, so that they blend into one another to create the water. Areas of trapunto and shadow Italian quilting can be used to form the rocks.

A close study of the back of a cat's head will soon reveal how the fur behind the ears will often part in areas, as suggested in the sketches in fig. 146. The richness and depth of the fur could be achieved by gathering a piece of panne velvet. The tubes could be held in place with reverse smocking and then lightly padded and moulded over a piece of pelmet-weight non-woven interfacing to form the head.

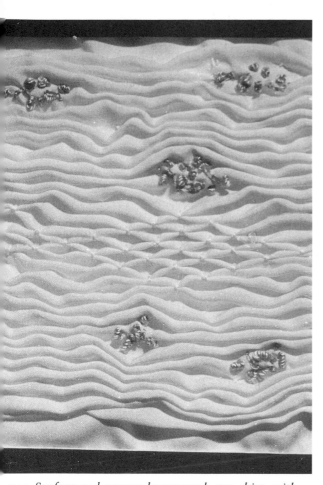

145 *Surface and reverse honeycomb smocking with added french knots could be the starting point for a water scene.* (Jean Smith)

146 *Notebook sketches suitable for smocking.* (Ros Chilcot)

147 *Random-dyed fabric which has been smocked, then stiffened by being dipped into a PVA solution and moulded into shape whilst still wet.* (Sheila Jolly)

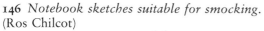

148 *A study of stone walling could spark off ideas.*

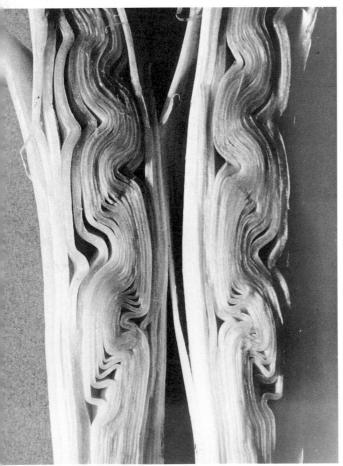

149 *Deformities found when cutting through a leek could be interpreted by means of smocking.*

150 *Frost on a window could make an ideal subject for further study and development.*

This could be attached to a suitable background fabric by working over the edges with herringbone or cretan stitch in the direction of the fur.

Throughout this book, examples have been described where smocking can be used to produce exciting and dramatic effects. Far from being exhaustive, these suggestions are intended to act as a 'springboard' by indicating the wide range of possible design subjects. The individual interpretation of a standard design by the skilful use of colour and technical merit, as well as the imaginative use of ideas related to personal tastes and interests, can produce a piece of work which is unique in every way.

151 'Flower Garden.' A variety of fine fabrics were gathered and applied to a canvas background. Some gathering threads were retained. Straight surface stitches have been added using assorted ribbons and threads to complete the design. (Ros Chilcot)

8 PROFESSIONAL FINISHES

It is a basic principle in all forms of art or craft that the professional finish can only be achieved by thorough attention to detail at every stage and by maintaining the highest standard of workmanship from the initiation of an idea to its completion. In smocking, the importance of proper finishing and neatening cannot be overstated. Carelessness in cutting or neatening an edge or in making up a garment can mar the intrinsic beauty of an otherwise perfectly executed piece of work. If the quality of workmanship fails at the vital finishing stage, no amount of remedial ornamentation can cover up the sub-standard work.

BIAS STRIPS

Bias strips can be used for many purposes, such as binding edges, covering piping cord and forming rouleau strips, as well as for a means of decoration.

Cut a piece of fabric on the grain, having first pulled the threads as a guide to help keep it straight.

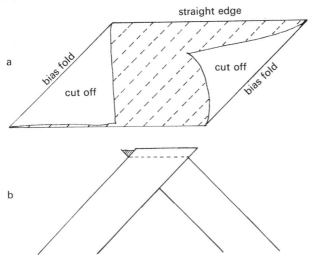

152 *Bias binding.*

Fold the fabric diagonally to find the bias, matching the grain lines. Cut along the fold. Mark lines with tailor's chalk or pins parallel with the cut edge at the required width for the bias strips (fig. 152). To join the strips, pin the slanting short ends with the right sides together as shown in fig. 152b, allowing the corners of each strip to project. Stitch, taking a 6 mm ($\frac{1}{4}$ in.) seam. Press the seam open and trim off the projecting ends.

BINDING SMOCKING

Using a matching thread and working on the back of the finished smocking, cable stitch along the top gathering thread. Cut a bias strip and, with the right sides together, backstitch the binding to the smocking, using the cable stitch as a guide. Trim the seam to 6 mm ($\frac{1}{4}$ in.) wide. Trim the top of the gathers at an angle with the highest part to the front. Fold the binding over and slip stitch in place.

PIPING

Piping is made by covering cord with bias-cut fabric which is wide enough to wrap around the cord plus an extra 1.5 cm ($\frac{1}{2}$ in.) either side for turnings. If a cotton piping cord is used, this should be pre-shrunk by placing in boiling water. Then proceed as follows:

1 Lay the cord in the centre on the wrong side of a bias-cut strip. Fold the strip in half over the cord, rolling it between thumb and forefinger to ensure the cord is snug within the strip. Pin and tack the strip with the wrong sides together and the raw edges matching.
2 Stitch by hand or machine as close to the cord as possible (fig. 153a).

a

b

right side

c

wrong side

d

153 *Piping:* (**a**) *fold fabric over piping cord and stitch;* (**b**) *piping placed on right side of first piece of fabric;* (**c**) *piping sandwiched between fabric and stitched;* (**d**) *joining lengths of piping.*

3 Place the covered piping on the right side of one edge of the garment or article. Tack in place along the stitching line (fig. 153b).

4 Place the second piece of fabric wrong side up on top of the piping, with all the raw edges lying in one direction. Snip the seam allowance up to the stitching, if the piping is to fit round sharp corners.

5 Tack through all the layers on the previous tacking line. Stitch by hand or machine (using a

piping foot) along this line (fig. 153c). Trim the raw edges to remove unnecessary bulk.

Where a continuous band is necessary, the piping should be joined before it is used. Measure the length of piping needed and join the bias strips. Unravel a short length of cord at each end. Trim each of the strands making up the cord to a different length, and then twist them round each other as shown in fig. 153d.

SOFT ROULEAUX

A rouleau is a neat way of making a fabric cord from a bias strip of fabric, made as narrow as the material will allow. It can be used for trimming or as a means of fastening, either as a button, tie or loop. It is often made in a contrasting fabric or colour, but avoid any fabrics which fray easily. Experiment with oddments of fabric to find the most suitable width for cutting the bias strips, because if it is too wide the rouleau will be soft and floppy; too narrow will make it difficult, if not actually impossible, to turn through. When the fabric is cut on the cross a rounded roll will result, and the seam will not be obtrusive.

Cut bias strips of fabric to the required width, joining them if necessary to produce sufficient lengths. Fold the strip wrong side out and stitch, using a slight zigzag stitch. The fabric is not tacked before stitching. Trim the seam allowance evenly, leaving enough to fill out the tubing.

Turn the strip by inserting an elastic threader, bodkin or large blunt needle and, using the ends of the machine thread, sew or firmly tie the eye to the turnings at the end of the tube (fig. 154). Ease the fabric on to the needle; take hold of the end and pull it through, turning the tube right side out. Cut off the needle.

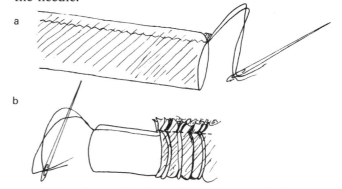

a

b

154 *Soft rouleaux:* (**b**) *shows fabric being pulled through to right side.*

CORD-FILLED ROULEAUX

For this type of rouleau a piping cord is inserted to give a more substantial result. Choose a thickness of cord that will be a suitable weight for the fabric being used and the effect required. If a cotton cord is to be used, it should first be shrunk by placing in boiling water. Cut a bias strip the same width as the diameter of the cord plus 2.5 cm (1 in.) for turning. Cut the cord twice the length of the bias strip. Starting in the centre and working outwards, fold the fabric over half the cord with the right sides together. Stitch the end of the fabric and cord together as illustrated (fig. 155). Stitch along the length close to the cord, stretching the bias strip slightly. Trim the seam allowances. Turn the rouleau by pulling the enclosed end of the cord through the tube, easing the fabric over the cord. Cut off the unwanted end of the cord.

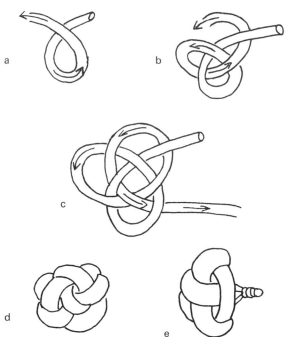

156 *Making a ball button:* (d) *shows finished button;* (e) *sideways view showing short shank.*

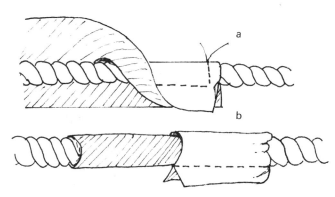

155 *Cord-filled rouleaux:* (a) *fabric stitched to centre of piping cord;* (b) *piping being pulled to turn the rouleau.*

HAND-MADE BUTTONS AND LOOPS

Hand-made buttons can give a charming and exclusive finish to a garment, and ensure an exact match to the background fabric or to the embroidery used.

Ball buttons

Use lengths of rouleau or thin cord to make the buttons, keeping them in proportion to the garment: the thinner the cord, the smaller the button will be. Allow approximately 15–25 cm (6–10 in.) of cord, depending on its thickness, for each button to be made. Carefully following the diagrams and directional arrows (fig. 156), form the button loosely, then gently ease the knot into a ball, making sure the cord loops in the direction indicated. A short shank can be made by stitching the two ends of the cord together and tightly wrapping with a matching thread.

Dorset crosswheel buttons

Using a thread of suitable type and thickness, according to the size of button to be made, buttonhole stitch all round a plastic curtain ring, pushing the stitches tightly together (casting) as shown in fig. 157a. Turn the stitching so that the ridge of the buttonholing is inside the ring (slicking), as in fig. 157b. Secure a new long thread with a firm backstitch at the back and wrap around the ring, moving the thread a little at each turn until there are between 8 and 12 spokes, depending on the size of button being made. Bring the needle up in the middle and secure the front and back spokes with a firm cross stitch where they overlap (fig. 157c). Work a spider's web from the centre outwards by backstitching over one spoke and moving forward two (fig. 157d). Variations in colour and weight of thread can give a very attractive effect.

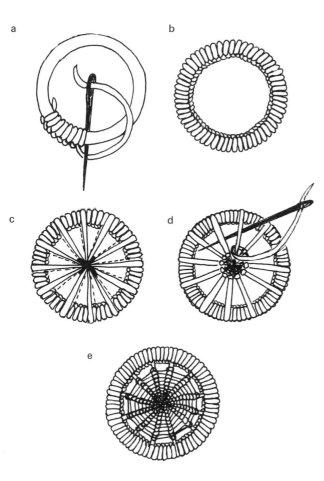

Fabric loops

Fabric loops are a decorative form of fastening made from a rouleau strip, and are generally used with covered, ball or other hand-made buttons. They can be used singly at the top of a slit opening, spaced out on an overlapping opening, or placed close together as a special feature. Ideally, the loops are inserted into a seam. However, if this is not possible they can be stitched by hand to an edge, although this is not a very strong method and should not be used where there will be excessive strain (fig. 158).

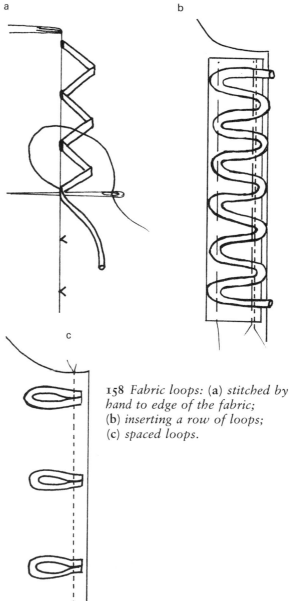

157 *Dorset wheel button:* (**a**) *casting;* (**b**) *slicking;* (**c**) *centre secured with a cross stitch;* (**d**) *weaving back one and forward two;* (**e**) *finished button.*

158 *Fabric loops:* (**a**) *stitched by hand to edge of the fabric;* (**b**) *inserting a row of loops;* (**c**) *spaced loops.*

Fabric-covered buttons

Plastic and metal button moulds in a variety of sizes can be purchased from most haberdashery departments. The fabric, which can be matching or a contrast to the article, is laid over the mould and clipped into place by means of a back plate.

Any form of embroidery or beading can be used to decorate the button, and is worked on the fabric first. To do this, place a piece of material over the mould and mark or tack around the circumference as a guide. Work the embroidery in the centre, and make the button up according to the manufacturer's instructions.

To insert a row of loops accurately into a seam, it helps if the rouleau is tacked to a piece of paper which has been marked out into equal sections. Make trial loops to fit the button until the exact length required is established. Carefully arrange the rouleau over the marks and tack straight down each edge of the paper. Position the paper on the right side of the garment, with the part of the loop that is intended to fit over the button facing away from the edge. Tack and then machine or backstitch through the loops, paper and garment, making sure the stitching is on the seamline of the garment (fig. 158b). Remove the tacking and gently tear away the paper. Place the facing of the garment right side down on the loops. Tack and stitch on exactly the same seamline. Remove the tackings. Trim away any excess fabric, but not the loops. Roll the facing to the wrong side so that the loops extend, and tack the edge. Finish the facing as usual.

If single or spaced loops are to be used, cut lengths of rouleau and carefully mark each one with the amount needed to go over the button. Place them in position on the right side of the garment, with the 'legs' of the loops together. The marks should be running through the seamline and the loops facing away from the edge (fig. 158c). Machine or backstitch in place and finish with a facing.

Thread loops

Thread loops can be used where buttonholes or rouleau loops would be unsuitable. They are not strong fastenings, but can be useful for edge-to-edge openings such as on baby clothes, nightdresses or neck openings, where they can look very attractive.

Use a double thread, and to avoid separation run it lightly through beeswax and knot the end. Take a small backstitch through the edge of the garment to secure the thread. Make a stitch equal to the diameter of the button, sliding the needle through the edge of the fabric to emerge by the knot and so form a long backstitch. Make three more of these stitches in the same place, checking as each thread is added that the button will pass through easily (fig. 159). Work close buttonhole stitch over the threads to complete the loop and fasten off by taking two or three stitches into the edge of the fabric.

INSERTION STITCHES (DECORATED SEAMS)

Insertion stitches are worked to join two pieces of fabric together in a decorative fashion, and can be most attractive when combined with smocking. It is important always to turn under and press both raw edges if hems are not to be finished at this stage. Tack both edges to thin card or cartridge paper, leaving an even distance between the edges in order to keep the stitches the same length.

Cretan or some other suitable insertion stitch may be used to join the two edges (fig. 160).

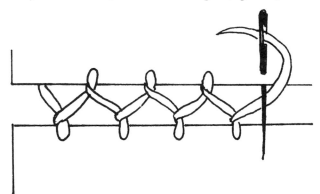

160 *Insertion stitches.*

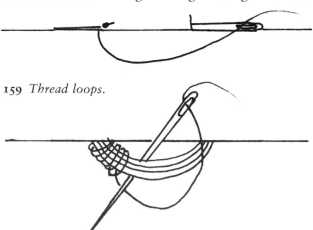

159 *Thread loops.*

136

HERRINGBONE STITCH

This stitch, worked from left to right, makes a very useful casing for elastic or ribbon, as well as being an attractive surface embroidery stitch. Catch up a few threads only, when working over the back of the smocked tubes.

161 *Herringbone stitch.*

TRIMMINGS

Attention to detail is particularly important, and can make all the difference to the final appearance of a piece of work. Collars and cuffs can have embroidery or suitable edgings worked in colours to match the smocking and give balance to a design. A few suggestions are as follows:

1 Oversewing the edge of the finished collar in one direction, then working back again, as shown in the dress illustrated in fig. 16.
2 Buttonhole stitch, or any of the variations, worked over the edges.
3 Herringbone stitch worked just in from the edge, as shown in fig. 106.
4 An evenly spaced row of french knots or beads.
5 Single, double or triple feather stitch, as in fig. 125.
6 Twisted chain stitch.
7 Cotton lace trimming with a thread matching one of the colours from the smocking threaded through the holes, as in fig. 13.

There are many other types of finishes and neatenings, not described, which can be used to enhance the smocking. It is essential, however, that the method chosen should complement and not overwhelm the technique, so ensuring that the beauty of the smocking is always presented in its most favourable light.

Index